Advance Praise for

Abe's Final Masterpiece

"One of the great masterpieces of our time. Every person looking to create perpetual success has to read this book."

~Steve Agentis, President;
Agentis Companies, Bethlehem, PA

"Mark's two year journey with Abe made the 20 life changing symphonies (principles) so easy to understand and enjoyable to read. A timeless classic that will be read and used by future generations."

~ Steve Schuman Partner,
Price Busters Furniture, Mid-Atlantic Region

"One of the best self-help books I've read: This book is a perfect example of investing in the right education; a pillar from Mark's chapter on the lyrics of learning."

~ Kathie Okun, President, The Okun
Financial Group, Hunt Valley, MD

"Every once in a while a book comes along with a powerful message, and shares it with you in a way you can understand and enjoy it. Abe's Final Masterpiece is one of those rare books."

~ Brian Layne- Founder/CEO,
DNA Life Bars

"One of the great seminal works of our time. Every person looking to create both professional and personal success should read this book!"

~ Alfonso Jimenez, President;
GDL Industries, Inc., Erie, Colorado

Abe's

Final Masterpiece

*'Inside this book, you will find principles
that transcend time and place.'*

Abe's
Final Masterpiece

*A Symphony of Lessons for
Business and Life*

By Mark Luterman

Based on a true story

Published by Primax Ventures, LLC - USA

Printed in the United States of America
Copyright © 2016 by Mark Luterman
ISBN: 978-1530249879

Editing: Heather P. Shreve
Cover art and cover design ©2016 by Heather P. Shreve

This is a work of creative non-fiction based on my life experiences. While my
story is true, it is not entirely factually accurate. My story represents a
combination of facts about my life. Names, dates, places,
events and details have been changed, invented or altered to
protect the privacy of the people involved.

Table *of* Contents

Author's Note

Two years. Twenty-four months. For some, this may sound like an eternity; to others, not long at all. That was the time I spent with a man I call 'Abe.' He took me under his wing and passed onto me 20 invaluable principles which changed my life forever. Every month, for about three hours, we met in the library of his New York City apartment (similar to the cover of this book). Those three hours were the most educational, enlightening, enriching and motivational moments of my life.

The truth is, it takes just about twenty-one to twenty-four months to truly embrace new habits, patterns, beliefs and values. This is based on The Four Stages to Unconscious Competency and the Trans-theoretical Change Model solidified by Dr. James Prochaska in the early 1970s. Basically, both concepts result in the same thing; **that humans learn and grow, and achieve mastery, in a predictable set of stages that are universal.** [My companion workbook addresses all of this and the twenty 'symphonies' in great depth. See www.markluterman.com.]

Most of us live in the third stage of competency: Conscious Competency, which means we *know* about the topic/idea/skill but we haven't *mastered* it...yet! Dr. Prochaska's model of change basically states that humans go through a five to six stage growth period until they reach the top of the mountain and can remain there. It looks like this: *I can't, I won't, I might, I will, I am,* and *I still am.* Again, most of us linger in the *'I will'* stage but never take the action required to achieve *"I am"* or higher.

This book will begin your journey to breaking through those stages and finally bust down those barriers which have caused you to hesitate! As I take you through this life-altering, amazing journey, allow yourself to be open to new ideas and philosophies, all the while dreaming big! Please know that anyone, no matter how much capital they have or how much education they possess, with the right mindset and attitude, can master these principles with sustained effort and commitment. As you read through the principles, please note that no *one* principle is more important than the other. They are all vital to your future long-term success.

I highly recommend taking notes and re-reading the material over the course of many months; two years ideally. This will put into practice the first law of learning: repetition, and cover the time needed to create **change that will last.** Additionally, at the end of each chapter, you'll find a section titled 'The Assignment.' These sections were the projects assigned to me at the end of each lesson and it was my obligation to complete these assignments and present them at the following meeting. I encourage you to complete these assignments as well so you can mirror the same path I took to achieve my desired goals.

So it brings me tremendous excitement to share and encapsulate for you this information. I know it will help you clear a path to greatness! My fondest wish is for everyone to achieve success in all things and to create a life full of unlimited health, happiness and prosperity so that you may pass it onto to future generations.

Mark

Introduction

I don't believe anything in life is coincidental or created by chance encounter. We design our own destiny. We attract what we think about most; we reap what we sow; we achieve what we conceive. We truly are the 'Masters of our Fate' and the 'Captains of our Soul.'

Back in the mid 1990's, I was a young CPA working in public accounting. After several years, at the age of 28, I attained a level of success most would find satisfying. Working with a wonderful group of diverse clients, we had created much success together. But, I began to feel burned-out from the long tedious hours of tax season and decided to venture out into the corporate world.

So I joined one of my clients, a young, small manufacturing company with loads of potential, to become a part owner and it's Chief Financial Officer. Armed with an array of tools which I had picked up during my accounting days, I mistakenly thought [as I was overly confident and cocky], I could immediately set the world on fire and help this company become an instant success; a leader in the industry of consumer products. Boy- was I wrong!

After about a year, I began to realize that running your own company was 'a horse of a different color'- a world away from advising others on what they should, or shouldn't do. Managing cash flow, dealing with employee problems, collections, keeping vendors current, manufacturing 'just-in-time' inventory, marketing with the right strategies, and creating a return on investment was a lot to juggle. Self-doubt about my abilities began to emerge. Underlying insecurities began to surface and I became hesitant to make the most basic decisions for fear of failing. Anxiety and depression lurked on the periphery; lost and adrift at times, I lacked direction and was unsure of where to turn.

Then, one Saturday evening my wife and I attended a wedding of a friend. During the reception, I was sitting quietly at my table and to my immediate left was an older gentleman. He turned towards me and looked right at me.

"Young man, you look like you're having as much fun as I am," he said in a methodical voice.

"Doubt it," I responded flatly, "I'm just counting down the minutes so that I can go home...,"

At that moment, it dawned on me that he was picking up on my melancholy; not my attitude about the wedding, but the story behind my obvious angst.

So he politely said, "Young man, my name is Abraham, but please call me 'Abe.' I'm here for the next three hours and aside from getting something to eat, I have all evening if you'd like to tell me what's troubling you, please do…,"

Normally, I wouldn't be so forthcoming about my problems, but something inside of me- a hunch, a premonition, a feeling of trust- reassured me that he was the right guy with whom I could safely share my issues. I started by introducing myself and telling him where I lived, [in Baltimore] to which he responded that he was from New York and related to the groom. After chatting a bit more, I started to explain how lost and confused I felt. I explained how transitioning from a secure position in public accounting to the world of entrepreneurship was throwing me for a loop! *And-* my experiences seemed to be that of 'failures' and setbacks. Emotionally I was disconnected and felt like I was at the crossroads of my life. It seemed futile. Without regard to how I sounded to Abe, [a man whom I had just met], I put all my cards on the table.

I continued to ramble on for the rest of the evening, and to Abe's credit, he just listened. He asked the occasional question which allowed me to share even more of my inner thoughts. After what seemed to be hours, Abe looked at me with a sheepish grin.

"I've listened to your every word and I can assure you that what you're going through is completely normal. In fact, many years back I experienced the same emotional instability you're experiencing now…and if you'd like, I'm going to make you an offer, which I hope will enrich your life so you can do the same for others."

I leaned in, now curious and intrigued. I wondered, *who exactly was I speaking with?*

"How can you help *me*? What words of wisdom can you offer in the next few minutes before we leave that will materially change my mindset?" I asked politely.

"Well, it won't happen in the next few minutes... but I'm going to give you my contact information and if you'd like to visit me in New York, I will be happy to share with you the many lessons I've learned over the years which helped me to achieve my defined purposes, " he said kindly.

We shook hands and I thanked him for his offer. I told him how appreciative I was that he spent his entire evening listening to my story.

Without hesitation, he looked me squarely in the eyes and said, "No- *thank you*, young man. Your story was heartfelt and I'm appreciative you shared it with me. Plus, it gave me an excuse not to have to dance with my wife and make small talk with distant family members, most of which I haven't the slightest clue what their names are!" I laughed, shook Abe's hand, thanked him once again and told him he would be hearing from me soon.

After the wedding I thought, *who was he and where did he acquire such wisdom to be able to mentor me? How was he qualified to help me?* I honestly didn't have an answer. Because I spent the entire evening talking about myself, I didn't bother to ask Abe what he did for a living, or even about his life. *Did he still work?* I assumed by his age that he was retired, but what did I know?

Once we got home, I immediately went to my computer to search for Abe on the internet. I pulled out his contact information and entered his name into one of the search engines. A whole litany of entries appeared! This 'stranger' [to whom I had been spilling my 'guts' to all evening] was an incredibly successful retired CEO from a major corporation and who had also spearheaded his own venture capital firm. It took me several minutes to process this information, but once I did, I knew I *had* to capitalize on this opportunity.

Two days later, on Monday morning, I called Abe right away and asked him how soon we could meet. I sensed a mutual excitement so we arranged our first meeting right then; I would drive up to New York City, about three hours from my home, and meet with him the following Saturday.

My journey was about to begin.

Symphony No. 1

The First Notes

"The very seed of success lies dormant
in the failures you experience"

It was 4AM in the morning when my alarm went off that first Saturday. I wanted to be sure I was on time, so I jumped in my car and headed north towards New York City. I looked at my watch: it was 4:30 AM. I was due to arrive at Abe's apartment by 9 AM. My excitement level was off the charts. In fact, I was so entrenched in deep thought about what I was about to experience, I lost track of my speed on the New Jersey Turnpike and got pulled over for speeding. When the officer informed me I was driving 15 miles an hour over the speed limit, I was brutally honest with him and explained why I was heading to New York. Incredibly, he let me off with a warning.

At 8:00 AM, I arrived at my destination. Not wanting to seem too eager, I waited in the car for about 45 minutes, which felt like an eternity. Around 8:45 AM, I headed into the apartment building and up to his apartment. I rang the bell and was greeted with a warm smile by Abe's wife. She invited me into this massive, elegant apartment furnished with items from the early Victorian period and then showed me to Abe's library. There was Abe, sitting behind a huge, very organized desk listening to a beautiful piece of operatic music.

"Come on in, young man! Welcome to my home. I hope you had a pleasant trip?" Abe said.

As I leaned over to shake Abe's hand I replied, "Well-except for the New Jersey State Trooper pulling me over for speeding, my trip was perfectly fine."

"Did he give you a speeding ticket?" Abe asked.

"No. Just a warning after I explained why I was traveling to New York," I replied.

"You're lucky", Abe said with a smile.

After chatting for a few minutes, Abe looked at me and said, "Before we get started, look around my study. What do you notice?"

"Thousands of neatly organized books..."

Abe then explained the importance of these books, how they were organized by subject. He said he had read every single one of them! Clearly, this was part of his success.

"Young man, I'm much more impressed with a person's collection of literary works than I am with any material objects they may possess. I want you to remember that. Are you ready to get started?" Abe asked as he went over to his CD player to turn off the opera playing in the background.

"I am... but would you mind leaving the music on?"

"Sure, are you a fan of opera?" Abe asked.

"I am," I replied, "and the aria you're playing right now, from the opera *Pearl Fishers,* sung by the duet of Jussi Bjorling and Robert Merrill, happens to be one of my favorite pieces."

I thought Abe was going to fall over. He was stunned I knew this particular piece of music as well as the tenor and baritone duet. I then explained how my father was a very well-known Cantor (a Jewish clergy who leads the service along with the Rabbi) and an incredible opera singer. I grew up with opera from a very early age so I had a real appreciation for this genre of music.

As it turns out, so did Abe, who requested that we carve out some time at the end of our session so we could continue our discussion on operas, singers and to learn more about my father. So, already we were reading from the 'same page,' maybe even the same note.

The First Notes

Abe took a seat behind his desk while I sat across from him with an open note pad and pen ready to learn and began the lesson.

"Mark, all your success starts with this first lesson. It is absolutely crucial you understand from the beginning that if you miss any one of the following five steps, any success you encounter will be fleeting. And here they are:

#1: You must have a clear and defined purpose.

#2: You must create a well-thought out, organized action plan [or blueprint] to map out the action required to achieve your clear and defined purpose.

#3: The most powerful force in the universe is taking right action in the present.

#4: You must have an unwavering, burning desire and commitment to accomplish your clear and defined purpose.

 #5: You must have an unrelenting faith and belief that you will accomplish your clear and defined purpose.

He proceeded to explain to me, in detail, these five steps…

#1: A Clear and Defined Purpose

Abe sat back in his chair and began. "When I refer to a *clear and defined purpose*, I'm referring to what you want to achieve, or what you desire in life. With a clear and defined purpose, you have the genesis of where every success starts. And I will tell you that you'll also become one of the very few in this world to have this clear purpose.

You see, the overwhelming majority of people- probably somewhere between 95% to 98% of the world- drift aimlessly through life without any concept of what they want to achieve. They do not have the slightest clue of what they want. There is no purpose, or objective, for them to strive towards. It's nonexistent.

And…I will tell you with great conviction that until you select a clear and defined purpose, you will spread your energies in so many directions that success will be impossible to achieve. An unfocused, unclear mind leads to weakness, indecision and ultimately, failure.

One of the most common problems you'll find with entrepreneurs is their lack of focus, or unwillingness, to stay the course with their main business. They're always looking for the next biggest and brightest shiny object that promises to deliver a stockpile of riches. Every project looks like certain success, so they keep chasing and chasing without ever achieving. There's a great book written by P.T. Barnum called *The Art of Money Getting.* Have you heard of it?"

"I've heard of P.T. Barnum but not the book," I replied.

Abe then went over to the section of his bookshelf where he kept his list of classic self-help books and retrieved *The Art of Money Getting.* He turned the pages as if he knew the exact section in the book he wanted to find. Then he read me the following excerpt:

"Engage in one kind of business only, and stick to it faithfully until you succeed, or until your experience shows that you should abandon it. A constant hammering on one nail will generally drive it home at last, so that it can be clinched. When a man's undivided attention is centered on one object, his mind will constantly be suggesting improvements of value, which would escape him if his brain was occupied by a dozen different subjects at once. Many a fortune has slipped through a man's fingers because he was engaged in too many occupations at the

time. There is good sense in the old caution against having too many irons in the fire at once."

He added, "Pay particular attention to the part that says…"

"When a man's undivided attention is centered on one object, his mind will constantly be suggesting improvements of value, which would escape him if his brain was occupied by a dozen different subjects at once."

He went on, "This suggesting of '*improvements of values by one's mind*' is called **The Principle of Self-Suggestion**, which we'll discuss in greater detail shortly. When you create your purpose, there are a few things I want you to remember:

First: You must be passionate about your purpose. Without passion, the road to achieving whatever it is you desire, becomes very difficult and tedious.

Second, you have an obligation to yourself to aim high. Don't ever settle.

Third, always set timelines to achieving your purpose. Don't let them be open-ended.

Fourth, you have an obligation as a leader to create clear and defined purposes and have the courage to support that purpose with action. When executed, your organization and surrounding members of your team will follow you're lead. Does this make sense?"

"Absolutely," I replied.

"Good. Now let's move onto the blueprint."

#2: The Blueprint

He explained to me that once you define you're purpose, you must create a blueprint to achieve it. The blueprint is your detailed step-by-step action plan; a roadmap which will lead you to your final destination. With this blueprint, there are several very important points to remember:

a) The more detail you provide, the more effective your action plan.

b) This is your time to think so stay focused. Stay away from distractions.

c) It is dynamic, not static. In other words, things never go exactly as planned, so be prepared to make changes along the way when you encounter a roadblock. The key is to make these changes proactively rather than reactively.

d) There is a direct correlation between the effort you invest in creating your plan and the time saved on "putting out fires" in the future. In other words, you're preparing yourself for success.

e) Your effort should be directed at accumulating as much knowledge as you can through education, such as reading the right books, your own experiences, research, and alliances with others you trust. These alliances are critical. You want to surround yourself with people who have achieved success and would like nothing more than to see you succeed. Their experiences, good and bad, can serve as a tremendous shortcut to achieving your defined purpose.

"So an alliance with a mentor such as you, Abe, is what you would suggest, correct?"

"Yes." he replied. "Many years ago, I was fortunate enough to have someone mentor me and teach me the philosophies and principles conducive to success and it helped me attain my defined purposes; then and now."

At that moment I was thinking; *I am so lucky to be sitting across from this man*. I saw this amazing opportunity to learn from a very wise and successful man. I would be hanging on his every word from here on out.

"Young man, remember, the person who vacillates in life, without a defined purpose backed by a blueprint, is analogous to a car without a GPS- and without good directions. Without either, you float through life without any real direction or purpose. But, the blueprint is useless without taking action," he reminded me, and he went onto explain why...

#3: The Most Powerful Force in the Universe

"The most powerful force in the Universe is taking right action in the present. Don't be indecisive. Indecisiveness is just another term for procrastination, **which is the deadly enemy of progress and success.** You can create the greatest action plan in the world; however, what good is the action plan if you don't act on it? Take action and if you fail, fail forward and fast, which is much more productive than remaining stagnant. When you fail forward and fast, you learn something new. We learn more from our "so-called" failures then we do from our successes. This learning process is necessary to help you find the right path to succeed."

"When you refer to 'taking the right action in the present,' how do you know what the _right action_ is," I asked.

"The right action is action that corresponds to the steps you've listed in step 2 of your blueprint ...and, most importantly, is done for the right purposes. In other words, the action cannot be harmful to any other person nor can it be illegal or unethical. This is violating the laws of nature and will ultimately be harmful and devastating to you. Does this make sense?"

"Yes...yes, it does," I replied

"Good, because it is important you understand step 3. Let me caution you that this is the first place most people falter. They complete steps 1 and 2 with the best of intentions but somehow step 3 acts like a steel barrier that stops people dead in their tracks."

"Why is that?" I asked.

"Upon the first sign of failure, what do you think most people do?" Abe queried.

"They quit!" I replied.

"That's right. They quit because they see failure as a final ending, as opposed to a learning experience. They don't realize that what they are doing is 'paying their tuition;' the tuition that is required to learn new ideas, concepts and philosophies necessary for perpetual success. And- in many cases- if they just went one step further, they would have achieved their defined purpose and experienced a successful outcome. This is why I estimate the overwhelming majority, somewhere between 95% to 98 % of people in this world, never achieve the success they desire. The limitations they experience in their life are self-imposed and that's very unfortunate. Because when you combine self-imposed limitations and a lack of accountability, you have the recipe for disaster."

Self- Imposed Limitations + Lack of Accountability= A Recipe for Disaster

"Mark, learn the lessons I teach you, and you will be part of the 2% to 5% who succeed beyond your wildest dreams. Now, let's move on to step 4…"

#4: Unwavering Burning Desire and Commitment

"If you really want to be successful, you commit 100% of yourself to your clear and defined purpose. Your desire to succeed will always be greater than your urge to quit. That's commitment. Also, remember that desire and commitment are not interchangeable. Commitment is a necessary component of desire. When you have a burning desire and commitment, failures don't deter you because you understand *the very seed of success lies dormant in the failures you experience.* You must have a burning desire to be great. You have to want to succeed beyond your wildest dreams. Your success is dependent on choosing your defined purpose and placing every bit of energy you have into making it a reality. It must become an obsession you are committed to attaining. Desire and commitment will also help you persevere through adverse and difficult times, which <u>will</u> occur. Anyone can commit when things are going well, but few will remain committed when adversity strikes. Deal with it, learn from it, and remain committed to your defined purpose. Now, let's move on to faith and belief..."

#5: An Unrelenting Faith and Belief

"You must have an unrelenting faith and belief in the process of accomplishing your clear and defined purpose. When you couple a burning desire and commitment with an unrelenting faith and belief, you'll guide your mind into believing it can achieve anything," Abe said.

Desire +Faith=your mind believing it can achieve anything

"But again, let me caution you here because this is the other area most falter. Upon failing and experiencing setbacks, self-doubt begins to linger in one's mind. Let me be very clear about this next point, a point I want you to highlight in your notes.

"Self-doubt is not an option and can never be present. If self-doubt exists, failure is a certainty."

"What causes self-doubt? Why is it so prevalent?" I asked.

"Fear and uncertainty," Abe replied, "fear of failure and lack of certainty; wondering whether your actions will result in failure. You see, most people have never experienced success in their life so it seems so unattainable, so distant. And because of their consistent propensity to quit upon the first signs of failure, it becomes habit forming. Their minds become programmed for failure and self-doubt immediately sets in."

"So, how do you stop this from happening? How do they break the habit?" I asked.

"By changing their thought process," Abe stated. "They need to see failures, setbacks and obstacles as learning something new, a necessary component to achieving whatever you want in life. *And,* by having the courage to continue forward through their faith and belief that success will be achieved.

Now, when you follow these five steps, your mind becomes so focused, so in tune to achieving your clear and defined purpose, you're rewarded with a bonus 6th step, the *Principle of Self-Suggestion.* I want you to pay close attention to this next part... and if I'm going too fast, please stop me."

The Principle of Self-Suggestion

"The principle of self-suggestion is the idea that our thoughts make suggestions to our subconscious mind which influence our decisions. When you create your clear and defined purpose in your mind, create a detailed step by step action plan, continually focus on taking right action in the present, have a burning desire to achieve it, and have full faith and belief in the process, it becomes the predominant thought in your conscious mind. These thoughts occupy the conscious mind and become the driver behind the determination to accomplish your goals. In time, that purpose is impressed upon the subconscious mind.

Think of self-suggestion as a communication link between the conscious and subconscious minds. The dominate thoughts of the conscious mind reach the subconscious mind and influence it with suggestions, whether they are positive or negative. Your subconscious mind, nurtured by these thoughts will then act upon them and supply you with ideas, concepts, strategies, and plans to help you achieve whatever it is you desire. I want you to prepare mentally for receiving these ideas and act upon them immediately."

"If this seems a bit esoteric to you, Mark, think about a time when an idea suddenly popped into your mind or you had that '*Ah-ha*' moment. That's the subconscious mind working to help you. It acts as a sixth sense. Or, have you ever experienced a time where you saw someone you were just thinking about? At a recent point leading up to that moment, that image, or purpose, was the dominating thought in your mind."

This was an entirely new concept to me, so it was taking me a while to completely understand it. I must have had a puzzled look on my face because Abe took a piece of paper out of the top drawer of his desk and drew me the following diagram:

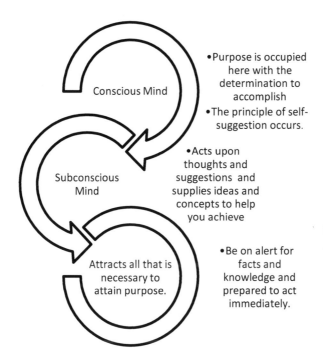

Conscious Mind
•Purpose is occupied here with the determination to accomplish
•The principle of self-suggestion occurs.

Subconscious Mind
•Acts upon thoughts and suggestions and supplies ideas and concepts to help you achieve

Attracts all that is necessary to attain purpose.
•Be on alert for facts and knowledge and prepared to act immediately.

"Think of your subconscious mind as a magnet," he went on, "when you follow the 5 steps, your subconscious mind will have a propensity to attract everything you need to realize your clear and defined purpose. But please remember, just as positive thoughts create positive feelings and results, negative thoughts can have the same impact in an adverse way. Your thoughts are very, very powerful. So positive thinking is absolutely critical. Am I making sense?"

"You are...but how do I apply the 5 steps and the principle of self-suggestion? Is there a particular format or process that works best?"

"Great question! And, yes… there is a particular format I refer to as 'My Success Statement' or 'Success Contract,' " replied Abe.

Abe then proceeded over to his book shelf behind his desk and removed two sheets of paper from the book labeled 'My Success Statement' and 'My Success Blueprint.'

"Young man, I want you take these statements and complete them. The first is your success statement, which encompasses the 5 steps. Put great thought into completing this, with as much detail as possible and then make sure you read it every day until it's memorized. Purposes and plans change in life so don't be afraid to modify it when needed.

The 2nd statement is your detailed blueprint. The blueprint takes your success statement and breaks it into components leading up to the deadlines you've set to accomplishing your defined purposes. That's why I want you to break it down month by month for the next 12 months. This is your roadmap and will allow you to stay focused consistently.

In order for us to be successful, we must create solid momentum and it begins with you completing this assignment. There is a lot of work here. Are you up to the challenge of completing this by next month's meeting?"

"Yes, I can't wait to get started!"

"Great. Now before we conclude today's session, I'd like to hear more about your affection for opera…"

Every night for the next four weeks, I would come home from work and delve into my success and blueprint statements. I was amazed by the thoughts and ideas that would randomly pop into my mind. I attributed this to my laser-like focus on my defined purpose. Now, I was seeing the principle of self-suggestion at work.

The Assignment
<u>My Success Contract</u>

My clear and defined purpose is to:

_____ [Example: a self-sustained business that will that will gross $_____ annually and create a net operating profit of $xxx by _____ (date).]

In order to achieve my clear and defined purpose, I will spend as much time as needed to_____

_____.

[Example: Grow my company with terrific, loyal clients that appreciate my solutions to _____. I will put their interests ahead of mine at all times, and I will always give them more than what they expect.]

I will do this with the following action steps:

    1. _____

    2. _____

    3. _____

I, _____[your name] will commit 100% of myself to making my clear and defined purpose a reality. My desire and commitment to succeed will always be greater than my urge to quit. I have full faith and belief in the process of accomplishing my clear and defined purpose and I will not submit to self-doubt. I will be prepared for plans that are supplied to me and will act upon them immediately.

Name: _____

Date: _____

Note: This success statement encompasses all 5 of the steps and must be completed. [Read this daily to impress your defined purpose on your subconscious mind. Make it your statement so powerfully that you accept this purpose as a path to success which will eventually dominate the actions and events in your life and lead you towards attaining your defined purpose.]

My Success Blueprint:

Month 1: _____

Defined Purpose[s]) for the Month:

    1. _____

    2. _____

    3. _____

Action Steps to support purpose[s]:

    1. _____

    2. _____

    3. _____

Symphony No.2

Take The Lead

"Lack of accountability represents one of life's greatest deceptions."

It seems like it was just yesterday, I thought to myself as I drove up the New Jersey Turnpike to meet Abe for our second session. One month had flown by! But, here I was - armed with my detailed success statement, the blueprint and a three year projected profit and loss- heading up to see him again. I couldn't wait to show him the work I put in to my first assignment. I felt rejuvenated by my action steps.

When I pulled up to his apartment building, unscathed by any speeding violations this time, I parked my car and took a few minutes to embrace this incredible opportunity. I was determined to put in whatever work was necessary to change my life for the better. As I walked into the library for our second session, Abe was sitting upright in his large leather bound chair, with a big smile on his face. Again, in the background was a beautiful piece of operatic music.

"Welcome, young man. How was your trip?"

"Fantastic, Abe. It's good to see you."

"I thought you might enjoy the aria playing," Abe mused.

"Of course I do. Is that why you're smiling?"

"Oh, yes! I went out and purchased this CD after our conversation at the end of our first session."

The aria he was playing, *Non Piangere Liu,* was from the opera *Turandot,* featuring the tenor Franco Corelli and soprano Birgit Nilsson. The aria, the opera and the tenor are all my favorites.

"It's amazing, isn't it?" I enquired.

"It is..." said Abe, "I've already listened to it a dozen times since we last met."

Listening to a variety of classical music was becoming a touch stone for us; something that had the potential to become a ritual at the beginning of each session. I could sense it would bring him great joy to try and stump me with his song choices.

"Okay, are you ready to begin?"

"I am..."

"How did your assignment go?"

Without saying a word, I pulled out a thick spiral notebook, divided into sections, and placed it on Abe's large Victorian desk.

"Looks like you've been busy. How do you feel?"

"Fantastic! I have a plan. I've begun to take action and I can see the principle of self-suggestion at work already and how powerful it is."

Abe then opened my spiral bound book and started to review my work. For the next hour, he asked me questions and made a few suggestions. Finally, he looked at me and said, "It's apparent to me that you put in a great amount of time and effort into this; it shows. I'm proud of you. It's one of the finest pieces of work I've seen …and if you continue on this journey, I promise you, you will be successful."

Beaming with pride, I thanked him for his kind words and assured him I would continue to work relentlessly on the homework he assigned me.

"Let's start today's session. Young man, there is a constant attribute in every entrepreneur that fails, without exception, and that is the entrepreneur unwilling to take responsibility for their own flaws, mistakes and shortcomings. I refer this as a lack of accountability."

Lack of accountability represents one of life's greatest deceptions.

"Do you know why it's one of life's greatest deceptions?"

I thought for a few seconds and responded, "Because you're deceiving yourself?"

"That's absolutely correct," said Abe.

"No entrepreneur can have enduring, consistent success until they look at themselves and discover their true flaws. This is the first step to being accountable. Recognize your weaknesses, your shortcomings, your limitations, so you can improve them and turn them into strengths. Life is a constant journey of improving yourself each and every day. The minute you stop learning, improving, trying to better yourself is the day you stop growing as an individual. Successful, content, and secure people, which I have surrounded myself with, are always looking to improve and learn things they didn't know yesterday. *And*, they never cast blame on others when things go wrong. This is being *accountable* and taking the lead in everything you do- for better or worse. This is being secure in your ability to succeed. This is the definition of a true leader and the very foundation of the underlying principles of true accountability."

He went onto say, "You'll discover, if you haven't already, that most individuals will blame others for their own mistakes simply because they're insecure in their own abilities to succeed in life."

"Abe, I have to admit, I may be one of those individuals. I've blamed others for past failures and unsuccessful outcomes. As I sit here, I can think of many examples that have taken place at work and at home."

"So starting today, you'll make the change," Abe responded. "This will be one of your assignments. I want you to list all of your shortcomings and the attributes you need to improve upon. And- be honest with yourself! Remember, lack of accountability represents one of life's greatest deceptions."

"I'll begin working on it immediately. I have a month to compile, what I imagine will be, a very long list," I said with a chuckle.

"We all have long lists," responded Abe with a smile. "That's why no one will ever reach perfection."

Leadership

"Now... as I just mentioned, the definition of a true leader is one that is always accountable. Accountability and leadership are never, ever interchangeable. Accepting truth and reality define a true leader. The best leaders of any organization, groups or associations are always prepared to accept setbacks without worrying where the fault lies, yet courageous enough to shower gratitude to those who helped cultivate a successful outcome. When you engage and create this type of culture, you're staff will be much more engaged and happy, and they will be compelled to follow your lead. And when this occurs, success is much more likely because you're working seamlessly together as one unit to attain whatever purpose or goal you've set." He explained that this occurs because:

a) You've earned the trust of your staff by setting the standard of true accountability.
b) Your staff will be engaged to work harder because of your gratitude and appreciation.
c) They won't be worried about making mistakes for fear of being blamed and ostracized.

I realized at this point how miserably I'd failed at creating this culture. My lack of accountability was one of the key components contributing to a lack of success. However, I was grateful for this lesson and the tools it was providing me, as I needed to make a swift change.

"So- for your second assignment, I want you to take the next month and whenever something goes wrong or you have a setback, I want you to think about what you could have done differently to change the outcome to a positive one. Additionally, when something goes right, I want you to shower praise and gratitude to all those involved. In both cases, compile a list and bring that list with you to our next meeting."

"No problem," I replied, "I can't wait to get started."

Master of Your Fate and Captain of Your Soul

"Before we conclude today's lesson, Abe stated, I hope you're beginning to see and understand that your future is entirely within your own control and is not dependent upon anyone else.

You truly are the master of your fate and the captain of your soul. You, and only you, will determine the fate and success you wish to achieve."

And with that, Abe walked over to his library shelves and pulled out a book of poetry. He turned the pages and asked me if I'd ever heard the poem, *Invictus* by William Ernst Henley. I told him that I hadn't so he began to read:

"Out of the night that covers me,
Black as the Pit from pole to pole,
I thank whatever Gods may be
For my unconquerable soul.

In the fell clutch of circumstance
I have nor winced nor cried aloud
Under the bludgeonings of chance
My head is bloody, but unbowed

Beyond this place of wrath and tears
Looms but the horror of the shade
And yet the menace of the years
Finds, and shall find, me unafraid
It matters not how strait the gate,
How charged with punishments the scroll.
I am the master of my fate;
I am the captain of my soul.

"Mark; be the master of your own fate, take full responsibility for your own actions, and never look to make excuses and blame others for your own shortcomings."

Now, let's talk about one of my favorite operas, **Tosca…**"

<u>The Assignment</u>

1) Make a list all of your shortcomings and the attributes you think you need to improve. Be rigorously honest with yourself remembering that lack of accountability can be one of life's greatest deceptions.

2) Over the next month, whenever something goes wrong or you incur a set-back, think about what you could have done differently to change the outcome to a positive one. Additionally, when something goes right, shower praise and gratitude to all those involved. In both cases, record them in a list.

Symphony No.3

Tuning In

*"The greatest opportunities often lie resting
in the most innocuous events."*

During the next month, I compiled a very detailed list of what I perceived to be flaws or attributes I needed to improve upon. It was intense but somewhat liberating. I felt, for the very first time, I wasn't deceiving myself, which as Abe said, was one of life's greatest deceptions.

My list included characteristics such as:

- Blaming others for my mistakes
- Impatience
- Lack of compassion
- Selfishness
- Anger
- Bad temperament

- Disregarding other's feelings
- Engaging in gossip
- Jealousy
- Greed
- Envy
- Insecurity
- Egotistical

When I finished my list, I realized how much work I had ahead of me to turn things around. Success would not be attainable without addressing these adverse traits. But I knew Abe would be happy to see the sheer honesty and transparency of my list. And…I knew that changing my actions and re-actions would help me to achieve my defined purposes.

For the second assignment, I recorded every event which did not end in a positive outcome and what I could have done differently to 'flip the script.' For example, one of my employees billed a customer incorrectly costing the company several hundred dollars. Instead of getting angry with the employee, I took responsibility for not having the right internal controls in place to catch the mistake. When I explained this to my staff, accepting full responsibility, everyone became more engaged willing to offer their opinion on how to avoid this problem in the future. I used this experience as a teaching tool for all involved. This change in behavior created a much more favorable and positive response.

Additionally, I used every opportunity possible to shower praise and gratitude to my staff members as well. Each day I would make sure to compliment at least one person on a job well done. Within two weeks' time, I sensed a dramatic shift in the company's culture. More people were smiling and there was less fear of making mistakes.

Walking into his apartment that next Saturday morning, I was full of anticipation; excited to share these results with Abe.

"Hello, young man. How was your trip?"

"Fine. It took me no more than three hours to get here, and as an aside, I must say your taste in music is impeccable!"

Abe smiled knowing where I was headed.

"The name of the aria you are playing is **Amor ti vieta** from the opera **Fedora** and based on the quality of the sound, from the early 1900's, the tenor is Enrico Caruso."

"Bravo!" laughed Abe, "I guess I have my work cut out to try and fool you…"

"Perhaps," I smiled, "Remember, my passion and interest is with tenors so if you play an aria sung by a *soprano*, the odds are in your favor."

"I'll keep that in mind, although it will be much more fun to stump you on the name of the tenor," he said. "Now let me ask you one very important question. What did you notice on your way up here today?"

"What do you mean?" I asked.

"During your three hour trip, you must have noticed *something?*"

Now, I was somewhat baffled. _Was there an accident or some major happening that I missed during my drive, a test or maybe the beginning of a lesson?_

Abe could see the confused look on my face so he smiled and said, "We'll get to that a little later. Let's see how you did on your assignment." I reached into my briefcase and selected the following lists:

a) True shortcomings and attributes I need to improve upon.
b) Every event which did not achieve a positive outcome and items/actions I could have done differently to change the outcome to a positive one.
c) Examples of showering praise and gratitude to my staff members.

Abe read through every word on each list and praised me for my honesty. He also noticed the wonderful examples of acknowledgement and gratitude I demonstrated to my staff members. When I explained the dramatic shift I witnessed in the company's culture, he was ecstatic.

"This is how true leader's lead," he said. "They don't lead by fear or intimidation or blaming others when things don't go right. Again- very well done."

"OK, young man, when you first arrived I asked you what you noticed on your trip up here. You looked a bit baffled and weren't sure how to respond, which of course, I expected. That's because most people drift through life paying very little attention to the present moment, thereby missing opportunities right in front of them. If you think back to your three hour drive from your home to mine, how much of that time was focused on your current surroundings such as the beautiful blue sky, the different types of trees, or even the names of the different rest stops on the New Jersey Turnpike?"

"Very little, if any," I replied, "in fact, most of the trip was spent daydreaming and I haven't the slightest clue how I got from my home to yours. My memory of the ride has some big blank spaces…"

"And that's the point of today's lesson," added Abe. You must be aware of your current surroundings because ***the greatest opportunities often lie resting in the most innocuous events.*** "I repeated the phrase and Abe picked up on my queue and explained what he meant by this.

"Opportunities are boundless and unlimited; *incredible opportunities* surround us each and every day; just waiting for us to claim them! They present themselves all the time, but you must be ready for them. Unfortunately, most are missed because people are not focused on the *present-* the 'NOW.' Our minds are consumed with past events, or thinking about the future. For example, let's take a random conversation with someone you meet at a lunch event…this person may be a perfect alliance for you; someone to add to your sphere of influence, yet all you see is a person in a suit with a nametag making small talk because you're thinking about what you have to do once you get back to your office. A potential missed opportunity!"

"I understand completely," I replied. "I am guilty of that exact example."

"Then you'll really appreciate this story," Abe went on to say.

The Genesis of 'The Prosperity Retreat'

"Young man, in my late 30's I was a board member of a regional business organization. Each year they had an annual luncheon for their membership, which exceeded several thousand. As a board member, I was committed to attending even though I was extremely busy at work. You see, I was in the middle of closing a very large deal that would have a significant impact on the future of our company. I anticipated spending approximately two hours at this luncheon. Now keep in mind, I could have spent these two hours distressed about all the work awaiting my attention once I returned to the office. But, I made the conscious decision to focus my attention on meeting new people, cultivating existing relationships and enjoying my time as best as possible.

The attendance was quite large. Each table sat ten people and they're must have been 150 tables. At my table was an older gentleman I'd never met before. He was quite boisterous and you could tell he enjoyed the spotlight.

During one of his conversations with the woman sitting next to him, I overheard him speaking about a group of other business owners with which he met with on a regular basis to discuss ongoing issues and ideas. He referred to their group as a 'structured alliance' which was an organized effort to support each of their businesses. It was like having their own outside board of directors with everyone working together to help each other succeed. I thought this was an incredible idea, one I would pursue immediately.

Young man, by simply 'being aware of my surroundings' and focusing on the present, one of my most lucrative and rewarding ideas was born. I called it *'The Prosperity Retreat'*. 'The Prosperity Retreat' was a quarterly retreat comprised of ten targeted, hand-picked CEOs, exclusive to their industry. Four times a year, we would travel to a remote and secluded cabin in upstate New York and spend a weekend discussing issues, topics and concepts, and then devise solutions in a cooperative effort. The resulting outcome was everyone refined their defined purposes.

As the group's founder, I facilitated our retreats in a very structured and organized way to keep us on track so that each member was given the full attention of all the other members. I'm proud to say that these retreats were directly responsible for the participating members, myself included, enjoying many years of incredible success and prosperity."

"How did you structure and organize these retreats?" I asked. "Did you have a specific process …that led to this initiative being so successful?"

"I did," Abe replied. "The process was developed over time and was exclusively used for these 'Prosperity Retreats.'

"I'd love to hear more," I said, "This is very exciting."

"Well, let's save that for another session…" Abe replied. "For now, let's finish discussing today's lesson."

Stay in the Present

"The four most important words I want you to take from today's lesson is, **'Stay in the Present.'** This is the key to being aware of your surroundings."

"I hear you, Abe, but this is one area I really struggle with…my mind wanders constantly. New ideas and being creative is great, but how do I stay in the present for any length of time?"

"Focus, repetition and persistence. You must begin training your mind to focus on the current moment. It's like anything else in life. It takes some work and effort but it will become a habit eventually. Remember; **focus, repetition and persistence** are the three key elements necessary for something to become habit forming."

The Keys to 'Tuning In'

"Here's what I want you to start working on to become more focused on the present. Consider this your 1st homework assignment this next month.

1. You must immediately stop dwelling on past events. They have no bearing on your future unless you allow them to. Whenever you find yourself in this thought pattern, remind yourself to stop.

2. Stop worrying about 'debts that most likely will never come due'. These are the negative 'what ifs' that most

people think about, which create negative wasted energy and anxiety.

3. While you should plan for the future, don't lose sight of how important it is to enjoy the moment you're currently experiencing. These experiences are directly responsible for helping you to mold the future you'd like to attain.

4. Pay attention and listen, listen, listen. There is a terrific quote from a famous Greek philosopher, Epictetus, ***"We have two ears and one mouth so that we can listen twice as much as we speak."*** Remember this because when you master the art of listening you'll provide yourself with a distinct advantage in life.

5. When opportunities present themselves, act immediately. Never procrastinate.

Abe went onto explain that most people are oblivious to life's everyday events and what is happening around them. That success can slip through your fingers if you aren't careful.

"Abe, I'll review this list every day to remind me how important it is to stay 'tuned in' to the present. This will be an enormous accomplishment if I can stop my mind from constantly wandering. It's one of my greatest weaknesses."

"Young man, to help you get started on forming the habit of 'staying in the present,' I want you to list at least three examples of opportunities you discovered from staying in the 'Now' before we meet again next month. Remember, at least three. Three is the minimum. What you'll find is that by 'staying in the present,' opportunities will present themselves every single day."

"I'll get started immediately Abe…"

On the drive home, I really wanted to start practicing 'tuning in' to the present. However, I was finding it awfully difficult. But, I had a good excuse; I couldn't stop thinking about Abe's prosperity retreats! Traveling to a remote location and spending a weekend discussing issues, topics and concepts, and then devising solutions in a coordinated cooperative effort really appealed to me. I wanted to start immediately but I wasn't sure how to proceed or how to facilitate one. Fortunately, I would only have to wait a few more months to learn more about the prosperity retreats. Once I did- wow! It would become the foundation for creating incredible success for myself and businesses all across the country.

The Assignment

1) Review Abe's list of 5 recommendations above. Read them every day for the next month until they become engrained in your mind.

2) List at least three examples of opportunities you came across as a result of being 'tuned in' to your surroundings.

3) Practice the acronym **W‑A‑I‑T**: Why Am I Talking? It will help you remember to be selective in your conversations and to leave others feeling <u>heard</u>. The impression you leave behind is more important than the words you use.

Symphony No.4

The Fearless Composer

"Fail forward, fail fast, but never remain stagnant."

Every day for the next month I reviewed Abe's 5 recommendations for 'tuning in to my surroundings.' After a few weeks, my mindset was shifting. My level of worry had dropped about any future events and I wasn't dwelling on past events either. The days became more enjoyable and my level of anxiousness subsided greatly.

I listened more and spoke less, which allowed me to hear **twice** as much as I did before. A simple change which was making a huge difference in the way I approached things. I learned of new and exciting ideas and opportunities. The way people responded to me was noticeably different because I was showing interest in what they were saying. They were starting to feel important and appreciated. And, lastly-when opportunities presented themselves, I acted immediately. Three examples came to light as I spoke with Abe that month.

After our customary greeting, we got right to session four. I began by telling Abe the changes which were occurring.

"Because of the assignment, I've started noticing things I never did before; I actually 'see' what is going on around me now…and it's becoming easier and easier because I'm able to stay in the present."

"Give me an example…" Abe suggested.

"Well, the other day I noticed the different names of the rest stops and service areas along the New Jersey turnpike. I never realized one of the stops was named after Vince Lombardi, the famous head coach of the Packers!"

"See…this is good!" proclaimed Abe. "Did you find your assignment helpful with discovering new opportunities?"

"Absolutely!" I said. "If it's OK, I'd like to start by reviewing three opportunities I discovered from this exercise."

"By all means, but before we proceed aren't you forgetting something." I looked around and back at Abe then realized I hadn't taken a guess at the current opera playing. I listened for a moment.

"I thought we were sticking to tenors. You're playing an aria sung by a soprano."

"I thought I'd mix it up a bit," Abe said with a sheepish grin on his face.

"OK, Abe. This aria is *Un bel di vedremo* from the opera *Madame Butterfly.*" Then I paused for a few seconds. "It sounds like… Maria Callas?"

"That's right." Abe said in disbelief. "I thought you didn't know female opera singers?"

"Well, I really don't, Abe, but I took an educated guess. This is probably one of the more famous soprano arias..."

"*Now* - it's 'on'- young man! I will stump you next month!" It felt good to be able to speak intelligently about a topic that Abe enjoyed so much.

"Alright then you have three opportunities you discovered from your homework that you wanted to share with me?" Abe still looked somewhat disappointed from not stumping me. So, I proceeded to pull out the following list, hoping to cheer him up.

My Discovered Opportunities

a) Business: As I was walking through our manufacturing facility, I overheard two of the line workers speaking about a glitch on our production line, which was slowing the number of products we were able to produce during a normal run. After approaching them about this issue, we were able to discuss other alternatives that cut our production time significantly, positively affecting our bottom line.

This was significant because normally I would be consumed with some other matter and would have paid no attention to this seemingly innocuous conversation.

b) Business: As a board member of a local Chamber of Commerce, I attended a luncheon where I was required to be a presenter. While attending the event, I initiated the conversation with a gentleman at my table as I noticed his name tag and the municipality he worked for. He was able to assist me in solving a very important compliance issue for our company.

This example demonstrates my awareness of the people around me. Normally, at most business events, I would find myself distracted thinking about the work waiting for me at the office.

c) Personal: Our family was attending a birthday party for one of our child's friends. As we pulled up to their house, I noticed how beautiful their yard was. I kindly asked for the name of their landscaper and subsequently hired them for our landscaping needs resulting in much better service and a tremendous monetary savings.

I assured Abe there were many more examples. These three were just a sample of how opportunities present themselves when you're tuned into your surroundings.

"This is great work," Abe said." As you can see first-hand, there are an infinite amount of opportunities available to anyone who wants them. You *just* have to pay attention and be aware. This sounds so simple but it's *the practice* and the actual 'doing' which eludes most people..."

"Okay, let's move onto today's lesson. What do you think is the #1 reason businesses and people in general, don't succeed?"

"Lack of a defined purpose and a blueprint?"

"Good answer- but try again."

"Lack of desire and commitment?"

"Nope, try one more time…"

"Procrastination?"

"Close, but still not correct."

"The #1 reason for failure is FEAR. I refer to fear as the 'silent business killer.' Fear leads to indecisiveness, which as you learned, is another word for procrastination. When you procrastinate, you defer taking right action in the present, which again [as you learned] is the most powerful force in nature. So, today's lesson is about courage."

The Fearless Composer

"Young man, I define courage as a willingness to confront your fear and continue to move forward and persevere. To overcome fear you must have an unwavering desire to succeed; no matter what. You must possess courage and an absolute belief and unrelenting faith your defined purposes will become a reality. When you combine burning desire with unrelenting faith, you own the ultimate recipe for success!

Courage is a mental attitude empowering a person to face fear without hesitation. The Fearless Composer is constantly moving forward, free from any worry, knowing that there is no failure, only learning. Missteps and setbacks will happen but when you are courageous, you're unafraid to keep moving forward. Choosing fear is just that- a choice. It's a choice that stems from your thoughts and how you choose to use them. If you choose and desire to be great, you will. If you choose to be fearful and indecisive, you will not fulfill your dreams.

Your success is dependent on choosing a definite goal, and placing every bit of energy you have into making that goal a reality. It must become an obsession which you can envision yourself attaining. With the right mindset and a persistent desire to succeed, anyone- no matter their level of formal education or experience- can succeed beyond their wildest dreams."

The Silent Business Killer for Business Owners

"Doing nothing is what I refer to as 'mental paralysis.' I use this term because so many entrepreneurs suffer from mental paralysis which results in physical paralysis. They feel stuck. They're not sure which way to turn, so they do nothing. Soon, even the simplest tasks or decisions become 'bigger than life' and difficult to tackle.

Although their stories are different, unsuccessful entrepreneurs have one factor in common; consistent and ongoing periods of stagnation and a lack of progress, which keeps them from achieving the success they desire. It can all be traced back to one common emotion: FEAR= False Evidence Appearing Real.

Fear is also a killer of your soul because you may be physically alive, but your soul is slowly dying from this debilitating negative emotion. Let me show you visually how this happens."

Abe then reached for a pad of paper and a pen to draw the diagram he referred to as 'The Cycle of Fear.' He explained to me this cycle occurs when one is afraid or fearful of moving forward in whatever endeavor they choose. Below is the concept he imparted to me:

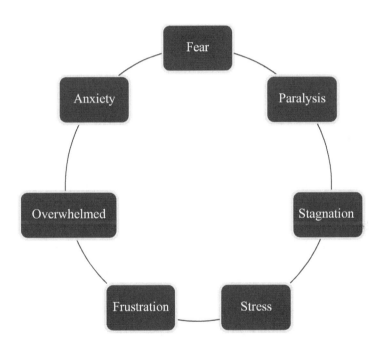

Abe went onto explain that he was not a licensed doctor or practicing psychotherapist but that his first-hand experience with counseling many entrepreneurs experiencing the same debilitating sequence had led him to this conclusion.

He added, "What I'm telling you, young man, is nothing revolutionary. We have known for thousands of years the incapacitating effects of fear, yet most people still allow it to control their lives. I want to read you something." Abe then walked over to his large collection of books, selected a book and read me the following excerpt:

"Having conceived of his purpose, a man should mentally mark out a straight pathway to its achievement, looking neither to the right nor to the left. Doubts and fears should be rigorously excluded; they are disintegrating elements which break up the straight line of effort, rendering it crooked, ineffectual, useless. Thoughts of doubt and fear never accomplish anything, and never can. They always lead to failure. Purpose, energy, power to do, and all strong thoughts cease when doubt and fear creep in."

"This was written approximately 100 years ago by James Allen in his book, *As a Man Thinketh*. This is just one of many examples of writings from many, many years ago referencing the adverse effects of fear." Abe then handed me the book and suggested I read it in its entirety. He then turned his attention to the power of decision making and the role fear plays in limiting decisiveness.

Your Absolute Responsibility to Make Decisions

"Everyone has within them the power to make decisions," Abe said, "Those that do make decisions are eventually rewarded with accomplishing whatever it is they desire. If you find yourself in the position of being in the majority, unable to make decisions for fear of failure or making mistakes, you must begin to form the habit of eliminating procrastination immediately. Remember: **Procrastination is the deadly enemy of progress and success.**

To eliminate procrastination, I want you to take at least one definitive action step each day towards your defined purpose. Continue this daily until you find your action steps are becoming habitual. Your assignment this month will be to keep a log of your daily definitive action steps. You'll discover that this practice will begin to create momentum and help you gain the necessary self-confidence needed to overcome the feeling of mental paralysis and stagnation. And remember, failures are an absolute necessity for attaining success.

It's important you always remember, Mark:

"Never elude your responsibility to make decisions. You owe it to yourself to continually move forward in business and in life and to be an effective leader."

Years later, I had the opportunity to pass those words onto thousands of listeners during a segment of my radio show; *'The Small Business Secret Weapon Hour.'* For three years I produced and hosted this live radio show heard weekly on CBS radio. It was rare that I was ever stumped, or at a loss of words on the show. However, on one particular segment I was asked a question by a guest that made me pause for a brief moment. The question was completely unexpected and unrehearsed.

He prefaced the question with, 'I don't mean to put you on the spot but…' This was followed by, 'How do you do it?' To which I replied, 'How do I do what?' He then asked, 'How do you consistently keep moving forward without ever stagnating?'

My answer was simple: **I never stop taking action.** Action is the most effective tool to combat mental paralysis and indecision. It can lead to a lack of decision-making and avoidance of responsibilities. The attitude to adopt is that any perceived 'wrong' decisions are really just learning opportunities. Unfortunately, the majority of business owners [and people in general] are consumed by fear, preventing them from taking responsibility for their decisions and taking the right action in the present, which is the most powerful force in the universe.

The guest started immediately taking notes, as did the show's production engineer. I also heard from many of our listeners after the show's conclusion how they were going to apply this philosophy to their own lives.

Living in Uncertain Times

Before the lesson concluded, I asked Abe about a particular type of fear; fear of uncertainty, or the unknown, and his recommendation on conquering it. [This fear was the one I obsessed about the most and created the majority of my anxiety.] Questions that spun around in my head were; *Will this work? Will I be OK? How will this impact me, my family and my company?*

"In today's world, there is a great deal of uncertainty facing everyone," Abe replied, "especially business owners. And this uncertainty is bound to cause people to react in two ways, at one time or another: to either retreat or remain stagnant. Managing this uncomfortable feeling of uncertainty and the unknown is not easy, so here are the steps I recommend…"

a) Attack the uncertainty by learning as much as you can about the issues causing your concern.

b) Don't dwell on issues you can't control; rather plan appropriately and prepare accordingly.

c) Commit your undivided attention to your own defined purposes and take the necessary action steps to acquire the success you desire.

d) With uncertain times comes fear. Let others be fearful while you remain focused on uncovering hidden opportunities that normally wouldn't exist.

e) Concentrate on creating new concepts and innovative ideas. When your mind is consumed with positive thoughts, it's too busy to worry about fear and uncertainty.

f) Have an unrelenting faith and desire that you will succeed no matter what.

g) You must remain calm. Your mind cannot properly think when it's in a state of anxiety and worry. Only when it is in a state of peace can it give to you the solutions to be successful.

"Young man, I recognize the most difficult of these steps is the last; remaining calm. Easy to say, not so easy to do. So here's a tool available to you at any time to help you remain calm in any situation. It's called the power of 'self-talk.' The power of self-talk is most useful when you utilize positive affirmations. For your assignment, I want you to come up with some of your own."

"Thank you for such a terrific lesson and advice...I will start using these tools immediately, Abe."

We said our 'good-byes' and I went back out onto the streets of New York City revitalized as usual. Although, this time, I felt as if I was drinking from a fire hose. This particular session was the most mentally challenging. I was completely exhausted from all the knowledge I was absorbing. So much so, I had to pull over at the Thomas Edison service area off the New Jersey Turnpike and rest for about an hour. But, no matter how exhausted I became over the next two years, I never forgot how lucky and fortunate I was to have Abe in my life.

The Assignment

1) Read the book; *"As a Man Thinketh"* [Resources Section]

2) Keep a log of your daily action steps with : Date -- Defined Purpose-- Action Step(s) Taken -- Outcome

3) Review the steps to effectively manage the fear of uncertainty.

4) Practice self-talk every day, see below examples:

✓ I've already succeeded. Now I'm ready to accomplish more.

✓ There are no limitations. The world is full of unlimited and abundant resources waiting for me to claim.

✓ I have the ability to think so I have everything I need to be successful.

✓ I live my life honestly and with integrity so nature will guide me in the right direction.

✓ Every day [and in every way] I'm getting closer to my goal.

✓ Every setback is just another learning experience necessary to achieve my final goal.

Symphony No.5
Behind The Music

"Discovery is a matter of investigation."

It was a beautiful winter morning when I arrived at Abe's apartment for our fifth session. "Good morning, young man," he said. "As always- it's great to see you…"

"Good morning, Abe. I'm ready, although I must admit last session was intense. I had to pull over at one of the rest stops on the way home because I was so mentally drained. We really covered a lot."

"We certainly did and we have a lot to cover today…" He smiled and said, "Listen to the opera- I think I got you *this time!*"

I listened to the aria for about two minutes, all while Abe was grinning from ear to ear; sure he had stumped me. He grossly misjudged my silence!

"It's *Un di all'Azzurro spazio* from the opera *Andrea Chenier*...sung by Mario Del Monaco."

Stunned, Abe looked at me and said, "But ...your silence? Why did you wait two minutes before answering? I was sure you had no clue and were stalling ...so you wouldn't have to admit you didn't know."

"Ahhh— I was just appreciating one of my favorite arias and giving you a false sense of victory! You see, growing up my father used to sing that aria in the house regularly. And, while I didn't appreciate it then, I certainly do now."

"All bets are off! *My* assignment this month is to find an aria sung by a tenor that you don't recognize!" I could tell Abe didn't like to lose, but, neither did I.

"I look forward to it, Abe. Now, let me tell you about my assignment...."

"Abe, I read *As a Man Thinketh* **three** times ...and I plan on reading it every year. Every time I read it, I learn something new. And, here are the affirmations that I came up with..."

Morning affirmation: *Today I am feeling healthy and vibrant in spirit, mind and body. I will enjoy every moment of today.*

Afternoon Affirmation: *There are no limitations. The world is full of unlimited and abundant resources waiting for me to claim.*

Before Bed Affirmation: *I've given my all and thank God for guiding me through a wonderful day filled with love, joy and happiness.*

"Every day, I also reviewed the steps to effectively manage the fear of uncertainty which you shared with me at the last session. After about three weeks, I found I was less stressed about future events and outcomes, which used to cause anxiety. I can see the power of habit and rituals is beginning to work.

To eliminate procrastination and avoid falling into the dreaded 'cycle,' I kept a very detailed log of my daily definitive action steps and I made sure to attack the most difficult action steps *first.* Over time, I felt more and more resilient which was allowing me to tackle bigger and bigger challenges. I reminded myself that any setback [or stumbling block] should be received with gratitude, not disappointment or frustration. I see now that setbacks are a necessary component of learning something new, which will lead to a successful outcome."

"Well done," Abe said. "You've certainly proven to me that you have a determination to succeed. Now, let's get started with today's lesson."

Behind The Music

"Discovery is a matter of investigation. And discovery can only be obtained from one of the simple, yet much overlooked traits that every highly successful entrepreneur embraces, **curiosity**. When you're curious, you look underneath things, behind things, looking for wisdom which will allow you to be creative and find solutions to achieve whatever you want in life.

There's a great physicist who said, *'I know quite certainly that I myself have no special talent; curiosity, obsession and dogged endurance, combined with self-criticism, have brought me to my ideas.'* I'm guessing you've heard of Albert Einstein."

"Of course-" I responded.

"Again, look around my library at the large assortment of reading materials. My love of learning and curiosity led me to this collection of incredible information, ranging from the self-help books to biographies of our greatest historical figures, to poetry, to world and U.S. History, and literary works from Shakespeare, philosophy, religion.... It's taken me many years to acquire and read this litany of books and it's one of my proudest accomplishments."

Curiosity Serves as a Protector

"You see these books— this vast array of knowledge— also helps protect me from propaganda and misinformation."

"How's that?" I inquired.

"Most people form their thoughts, opinions and judgments through what other people say or think. They treat this information as gospel without researching or exploring for themselves. It's a very lazy and incorrect way of educating yourself. One of the very first things I said to you was that I'm much more impressed when someone has a library full of books

___ *Abe's Final Masterpiece* ___

rather than a houseful of material possessions. I am not impressed with the latest gadget, like a new 60 inch color TV with all the bells and whistles…Television is just another vehicle that's filled with sensationalized and exaggerated stories which induce you to watch programs so that the networks can increase their ratings and sell more advertising. Unfortunately, this is where the majority of people receive their education.

And… because sensationalisms works, most stories you see on TV are negative in nature, based around corruptions, scandals and immoralities. I highly recommend you stay away from television as it will influence your mind negatively with unproductive thoughts. In fact, I never take anything I've heard at face value. I form my own thoughts and opinions from my own investigation and exploration. It's served me well as it will for you too."

"Abe, again, I have to put myself in this category. With all the information I have to process, and the overwhelming amount of tasks I have to complete each day, sometimes I find it easier just to accept someone's word for it and run with it. I realize now, this is a lazy and irresponsible way of thinking."

"Investigate, ask questions and investigate some more," Abe emphasized. "That's what successful people, and leaders, do. In fact, you should carve out fifteen minutes a day to investigate and learn something new *every day*; And, preferably towards your defined purposes. This should not be just confined to your defined purpose of creating a successful company. You should also investigate topics that pertain to enriching you and your family's personal life as well. Let this be part of your next

74

assignment; searching for knowledge, both personally and professionally. Make sure you commit yourself completely to this time and don't let your mind wander off onto other tasks. Those tasks will still be there for you to complete when you're done with this exercise.

Your second assignment will be to keep a log of what you investigated [or were curious about] for the next month so you develop the habit of completing this exercise daily."

"I'll start today... as soon as I get home," I replied.

Abe's $500,000 Discovery

"Now, I want to share with you a story of how curiosity led to a discovery of over $500,000. Many years ago, when I was your age, a dear friend of mine started his career in sales for a packaged goods supplier. The company had a sales force of five; four of which had been with the company for at least 10 years. My friend was the fifth; hired to replace one of the salespeople who had just retired. All of the accounts held by the retired salesman were distributed to the other four tenured salespeople. After they reviewed the list of accounts, they could either keep the account or turn it over to my friend. As you can imagine, the four salespeople picked the easiest and most lucrative accounts and left the remaining underperforming accounts to him.

He was new and had to begin from scratch, so he was eager to receive these accounts, without judgement and determine how he could cultivate these accounts into larger and more lucrative pieces of business. The first thing he did was begin to investigate why these accounts were underperforming. So he instantly scheduled appointments with the owners of these companies to introduce himself as the new salesperson.

After meeting with each one individually, he discovered that the retired salesperson would rarely call on them and, because of his lack of attention, the majority of their business would go to the so-called competition. He also discovered that each of the owners were very much alike, high maintenance, requiring a lot of attention and acknowledgement.

It became apparent that the retired salesperson wasn't interested in the hard work required to service these accounts, so naturally, the accounts underperformed. The other four remaining salespeople knew this from their conversations with the retired salesperson and decided they weren't interested in dedicating the time necessary to properly servicing these accounts. They formed their opinions solely on the retired salesperson's opinions and judgements.

Armed with enthusiasm and drive, my friend immediately went to work on providing the best service he could to each of these accounts and within a few short months he saw a sharp increase in the volume they ordered from his company. Here's where the story gets really interesting. One day, he paid a surprise visit to the one account requiring the most attention. His consistent commitment and attention towards this particular owner left a positive lasting impression so he was well-received whenever he visited. Feeling secure within the relationship, he approached the owner of the company and asked about a big warehouse sitting about 100 feet behind the manufacturing facility, one which he'd never visited. He was, in fact, curious.

The owner of the company told him it was the warehouse for all their packaging components and asked him if he'd like a tour. He was thrilled to have the opportunity and they spent the next thirty minutes touring the warehouse. During these thirty minutes, my friend took copious notes on all the different SKU's [Stock Keeping Unit] of product he believed he could service.

Upon their return to the manufacturing facility he turned to the owner, handed him a summarized sheet with all of these products listed, and asked if he could have the opportunity to provide him with a competitive price. The owner was more than willing to oblige.

Within 48 hours, my friend hand-delivered a price list of items to the owner. Some prices were lower, some were about the same. However, because of his commitment, dedication and desire for great service, he received a commitment from the owner to handle everything; which came to more than $500,000 dollars annually!

His curiosity served him well. He became the #1 salesperson within two years in the company. Ten years later, he became president of the company. He eventually grew the business to become one of the largest distributors of packaging and consumer product supplies on the east coast."

"Abe, this example has really motivated me to start spending the necessary time forming my own thoughts and being curious whenever possible. I'll start today."

"Very good, young man. You'll find a whole new world of discovery is awaiting you."

And he was right. I became obsessed with being curious over the years subsequent to this lesson and what a difference it made! Every day, I discover something new and exciting based upon my own research. Investigate, keep asking BIGGER questions, turn over every stone, look underneath the surface… keep looking until you find the answers you seek. These are words I've never forgotten and I continue to live by.

The Assignment

1) Find 15 minutes a day to investigate something that will enrich your knowledge personally and/or professionally. Make sure you commit yourself completely to this time and don't let your mind wander on other tasks you have to complete.

2) Keep a log of what you investigated or were curious about for the next month to insure you develop the habit of completing this exercise daily.

Symphony No.6

Setting the Stage

*"People tend to feed off of other's negative experiences.
It makes them feel better."*

As I walked into Abe's apartment this particular Saturday morning, our sixth meeting, I was greeted by a man who had only one thing on his mind.

"Good morning! Forget everything else, listen to the aria…"

I stopped and listened. After about thirty seconds, I turned to Abe and said, "I have some good news and some bad news."

"Give me the bad news first, young man."

"The bad news is the aria is *Chella Mi Creda* from the opera '*La Fanciulla del West*'….

Abe sighed, "And, the good news?"

"You got me Abe. I can't make out the tenor."

"Not even a guess?"

"Nope- you got me. Who is it?"

"Jan Peerce!" Abe blurted out in a victorious voice.

I sighed and said, "Shoulda gotten that one…"

"You've heard of him?" Abe seemed shocked.

"I have, Abe. Jan Peerce, like my father, was a Cantor."

"I didn't know that."

"Yup."

"You don't like to lose either, do you, young man."

"Nope!"

"OK, well- I'll relish my victory after you leave."

"Thank you. Now that you've stumped me, is it 'game over'?"

"It is indeed, but even though I am going out on top, we can still have fun listening to opera after our sessions are over."

"Smart. I would have nailed the next twenty," I said laughing. Abe was still chuckling as we began our session.

"Has your curiosity been piqued this past month?"

"It has. This past month was a real revelation."

"Please, tell me about it…"

"I've discovered more in the past month than I have in the past five years! I constantly have an urge to question and seek answers to things rather than just accept them at face value. Every day, usually in the evening, I spend at least 15 minutes investigating something that adds to my personal or professional knowledge. I read books and publications, and listen to CD's on philosophy, business, the power of the mind, music, history, family matters, financial investments, just to name a few! I am constantly inquiring about topics and subject matter which I wasn't well- versed in before. I really look forward to this now. Does that make sense?"

"It makes a lot of sense and it will only escalate in the future. You'll become addicted to learning and seeking knowledge, in perpetuity, which is a trait of all successful, independent people."

"Abe, I would like to share one example of discovery from being curious that I think you'll find very interesting."

"Please -share..."

"I've been reading a book I first saw in your library, the *Law of Success* by Napoleon Hill. In the chapter on the Power of Enthusiasm I came across the most intriguing quote on the side of one of the pages, which said, '*I gave a beggar a dime with the suggestion that he invest it in a copy of Elbert Hubbard's A Message to Garcia.*' In the past I would have skimmed over the quote and continued reading. However, I was so curious why the author would give a beggar a dime and tell him to read *A Message to Garcia.* I asked myself; *what is A Message to Garcia?*"

Before I continued, a knowing smile came across Abe's face. "So, I researched *A Message to Garcia* and discovered it was one of the great literary works, an essay, selling millions of copies and translated into many different languages. I also discovered it is still used by some members of the military to educate on the importance of taking initiative. *And* ...did you know it was first made as a silent film in 1916 by Thomas Edison?"

"That, I did not know. That's a very interesting piece of information that I will research. I'd like to know more about that. Did you read the essay?"

"I did. I was captivated by the lessons of initiative, responsibility and self-discipline."

A Brief Summary of the Essay
[Essay can be downloaded at www.markluterman.com]

The lessons I reference above are crystalized through the story of the Spanish-American War. In 1898, the Americans were preparing to invade the Spanish colony of Cuba so they wanted to quickly communicate with the leader of the Cuban insurgents, Calixto Garcia. Garcia was somewhere in the mountains of Cuba, but no one knew where.

The President at that time was William McKinley. In order to track down Garcia, it was suggested to McKinley that he call for an American officer by the name of Andrew Rowan. Rowan was sent for and given a letter to be delivered to Garcia.

McKinley was content that his instructions were transparent, and did not supply Rowan with any strategic advice or tips. He was confident in Rowan's abilities to locate Garcia. So Rowan took the letter without asking *'Where is he?'* After three long and tedious days of traveling in hostile country by foot, he found and delivered the letter to Garcia.

"I'm really proud of you. What a great example from your assignment. Remember to pass this knowledge on to others as well. It's a tremendous, but worthwhile, responsibility."

"I will, Abe."

"Okay- let's now move on to lesson 6:

Setting The Stage

"The influences we receive from our environment are critical to achieving success in business and in life. In order to 'set the stage' in your environment you must surround yourself with people and allies that create a positive atmosphere, inspire you and are willing to help you achieve your defined purpose. First and foremost, each person should be of great integrity possessing the highest and utmost character in every facet of their life. Without this attribute, nothing, and I mean *nothing else matters!*

Each person should also be passionate about their goals and purposes, and as confident and determined to succeed and persevere as you are. This is important because those that continue to strive to be better and succeed are rarely, if ever, envious of others who do the same. They're confident enough in their own abilities to achieve happiness based upon their own experiences rather than achieve happiness through other's failures. When you surround yourself with these people, you'll experience a mutual admiration and respect, in which each of you will encourage the other to succeed as well as help you to achieve your defined purposes. You should also strive to be that person who people are attracted to and want to have in their circle as well, possessing all the attributes and traits I just mentioned."

As Abe was espousing these points, I could see a new kind of passion emanating from him. Up to this point, he had been rather cool in his delivery of our lessons. This was different. This subject matter seemed to really 'strike a chord' with him. It appeared he was relaying a message from personal experience; an experience he was reliving through every word he spoke.

"Abe, I can see the passion you have for this subject. It's almost like you're reliving it....from past experiences that you went through to learn the importance of setting the stage."

"You are very astute! I did, in fact, learn the hard way about setting my own stage ..."

Setting the Stage: ACT I.

"When I was in my late twenties, I was married and had three young children, but I had an urge to start my own company rather than work for someone else. It was, as it always is, a calculated risk; one I believed would pay off in the long run. Aside from my wife, everyone I knew, including my own parents discouraged me from following my dream. They were telling me to keep the steady salary I had...and how irresponsible it was of me to put my family at risk. That was not the feedback I expected, or was looking for. In fact, all it did was create more angst and elicit negative thoughts. Although I couldn't remove them from my life, I didn't respond when the subject was brought up in future conversations. Looking back, this lesson proved to be of great value for I learned **never to defend against negativity**."

"What do you mean exactly, Abe?"

"It means when someone doubts you, or provides you with negative feedback that is not constructive in nature, listen, smile, move on and never defend because the minute you defend your position, you open the doorway to a conversation that is of no value to you. All you will hear is every reason why this n' that won't work and how you're wasting your time. In some instances, it may be said out of care from a parent or relative, but in most instances, it's done out of envy and jealousy from someone who doesn't wish to see you succeed. You owe no one, other than your spouse of course, an explanation as to why you choose the path you've taken."

"I see how this is starting to all come together, Abe. Trust your own instincts, be accountable for your own actions and if you fail or incur a setback, utilize it as a necessary learning experience that will take you one step closer to your defined purpose. And of course, throughout the whole process, relinquish the self-doubts and fears, which only serve to create your own self-limitations."

"Yes, you should trust your instincts and not listen to the negativity. But sometimes your instincts may be wrong. Remember how I emphatically stated that each person you surround yourself with should be of great integrity possessing the highest and utmost character in every facet of their life because without this attribute, nothing else matters?"

"Yes, of course…" I responded.

"Well, I learned this lesson the hard way, from a first-hand experience and this is why I'm so emphatic about the importance of one's character."

Setting the Stage: ACT II.

"I initially started my company with an associate of mine who I befriended right out of school. We started our careers together working for the same company. Our goals were very similar, to be independent and conquer the world. We were confident and believed [together] we were unstoppable. When we first started our company, everything was going very smoothly. My partner and I were growing rather quickly. We were attaining a level of success that was beyond our initial expectations.

After about three years, I noticed a slight change in his demeanor. He was becoming distant and aloof, going on meetings and not conveying or communicating the results and outcomes of these meetings. And when I would press the matter and ask for updates and status reports, all I would receive was excuses and idle promises that he would get back to me. So, I became curious. I contacted a few of the parties he met with and discovered that he had created a separate company and was depositing the funds generated from these new accounts into his newly created company. In addition, he was syphoning money out of our company, which he claimed were reimbursements for travel and client expenses."

"So what did you do?"

"I hired an attorney, dissolved our company and pursued an unnecessary legal battle with him that lasted for over a year and cost me tens of thousands of dollars in attorney fees.

Finally, I came to the realization that all of this acrimony and anger was accomplishing nothing but negative energy and a loss of focus on my defined purpose. I was off course, stagnating, and the only one I was hurting was myself and my family. I regrouped, called off the lawsuit and started to build my company with an urgency, focus and determination unparalleled to any other time in my life.

The ley lesson I learned, and I want you to listen carefully and heed my advice, is never allow anger to dictate your next course of action. Anger is one of the most damaging and harmful emotions that will stop any success from occurring because the only one you're hurting is *yourself.* If you think you're hurting the other party, you're wrong. Forgive, forget and move on. Learn from your mistakes and use it as a necessary lesson that will help you succeed in the future. Allow nature to take care of any transgressions perpetrated by the other party. In time, they'll receive their just due."

"Thanks for sharing that story with me…it's one of the most valuable lessons I've ever heard, and I will heed your advice and remember it whenever I'm in an acrimonious situation."

Setting the Stage: ACT III.

"Let's summarize this lesson so you can remember how to control your environment and set the stage in every facet of your life…"

1) Always remember the importance of creating an **alliance** of people who will assist you in achieving your desired goal. These individuals should be carefully chosen based on their experience, knowledge and for their ability to inspire positive thought. When you surround yourself with these people, you'll experience a mutual admiration and respect, where each of you will encourage the other to succeed helping you to achieve your defined purposes.

2) **Character** is the foundation of every great individual. Each person should be of great integrity possessing the highest and utmost character in every facet of their life. Without this attribute, nothing else matters!

3) Each person should also be **passionate** about their goals and purposes, confident and determined to succeed and persevere. This is important because those that continue to strive to be better and succeed are rarely if ever envious of others who do the same.

4) Don't forget to strive to be a person that others want to surround themselves with possessing all the attributes and traits we've discussed.

5) Remove every influence from your environment that elicits negative thoughts. I refer to this as 'toxicity.' Toxic people will act like an anchor to your defined purposes, always finding fault with something, or someone. Go back to our second lesson of accountability. Toxic people are the

antithesis of accountability, living a lie of deception and fraud.

6) Understand and be aware that a person's negative comments are just a reflection of their own weaknesses, shortcomings and insecurities. This mindset is pervasive and is the norm with the majority of the people you will encounter in your life.

7) Be confident and rely on your thoughts and hunches. This is a critical point, one which will cover in a few months.

8) Be immune to criticism. You will never thrive unless you have thick skin. Believe in yourself and believe that the path you're taking is correct. Do not worry what others think unless it's someone trying to help you achieve your goal.

"Have a safe trip back. I'll see you next month."

The Assignment

1) List all the people you know that you believe would make a terrific alliance. Follow the guidelines we just summarized and think about how each can become part of a mutually beneficial long-term alliance.

2) Make a list of all the people currently in your life that are negative influences and should be removed from your life. If you find you cannot remove them because they are family members, remember to listen, smile, move on and never defend.

Symphony No. 7
The Lyrics of Learning

"Neglecting to broaden your view will keep you doing one thing the rest of your life."

When I first received my last assignment, I thought it would be a breeze. It seemed so simple. But it wasn't. When you really take the time to think about how many high character, positive, non-judgmental, secure people there are in your life, who want nothing more than for you to succeed, the list ends up being a lot shorter than you initially think.

So I completed my list and felt fortunate for the people I believed could become a part of a mutually beneficial long-term alliance. [All the while, in the back of my mind, I envisioned our alliance participating in one of Abe's prosperity retreats. I wanted to re-visit this topic at our next session because I really wanted to know how to plan, organize and facilitate these retreats.]

Next, I had the unenviable task of listing all the people who were a negative, toxic influence in my life and should be removed. This list was the antithesis to my first list; surprisingly much longer. But nonetheless- I was prepared when Abe and I met next…and one of my wishes was about to come true. After our initial greetings, Abe jumped right in.

"Today I have a very special treat for you—"

"What's that?" I asked expectantly.

"In our third lesson we briefly discussed one of the major reasons for my success, my prosperity retreats. I vividly remember how excited you were to learn more about this topic, however, I asked you to be patient and wait until we cover it in a future session. Well, your patience has paid off! We will be discussing, in detail, this incredible strategy and how, if performed correctly, it will help propel you and your alliances to great success."

"Abe, I've been waiting for this moment with great anticipation and quite frankly, I intended to ask you if we could discuss these retreats in today's session. Thank you, and what a coincidence…!"

And before I could finish the word *coincidence*, it hit me. *This was no coincidence; especially from someone like Abe.* The last lesson and assignment [of creating an alliance of carefully chosen high character, positive, passionate people who will assist me in achieving my desired goal, where each of us will encourage the others to succeed to achieve our defined purposes] was done with the intention to prepare me for this lesson. And it did!

Abe asked me, "Before we begin our lesson, how was your assignment?"

"Enlightening," I responded. "I thought it would be so simple. But it wasn't. My list of successful people was a lot shorter than I imagined while the list of negative, toxic people was surprisingly much longer. The disparities between the two were quite significant. On one side, I saw an aircraft lifting off to great heights representing the positive influences, while on the other, a cargo ship docked at sea with a large iron anchor representing the negative, toxic influences."

"What a great analogy. Your imagination will serve you well in life."

Now for today's lesson, neglecting to broaden your view will keep you doing one thing the rest of your life. You've heard me refer to the importance of attaining knowledge. Again, look around this library. I consider this collection of literary works, which I've compiled and read over more than fifty years, one of my greatest and proudest accomplishments. The hours spent digesting these materials were fruitful; producing organized knowledge leading me to achieve whatever defined purpose I set for myself.

Remember, without an organized, well thought out plan, you float through life without any real direction or purpose. To ensure success, you must have plans, which are flawless. To create these plans, it is vital that you engage in accumulating as much information, facts, and knowledge as possible towards the achievement of your defined purpose. This knowledge will lead to independent thoughts, creativity, ingenuity, and provide the confidence you will need to take the 'right action in the present.' Independent thinking, young man- **this is where it all begins**!"

And with those words, I once again gazed around his library in complete awe. *How magnificent a picture!* A well-organized masterpiece of literary works, all at his disposal. A true lifetime achievement; more impressive than any material objects I've ever seen to this day.

Abe's Guide to The Lyrics of Learning

"First, let's start with the most underrated and under-appreciated way you will accumulate knowledge, **through your own experiences**. This type of education can never be replicated. It is essential, and when used correctly, will provide you with a lifetime of the greatest and most useful skills. I refer to these experiences as *Paying your Tuition*."

"What does that mean?" I asked. "And why is it underutilized?"

"First, 'paying your tuition' are the failures you experience," Abe replied. "Every time you fail, you learn something new, which is knowledge. This 'learning through doing' is the tuition you have to pay in order to succeed. It is much better to fail forward and fast than it is to remain stagnant. When you fail forward, you're actually succeeding in finding different ways to solve a problem.

So I want you to remember this the next time you make a mistake where money is involved. The loss of money is the tuition you had to pay to learn a valuable lesson, no different than paying money to go to a university, a trade school, continuing education or taking an online course. This lesson is a key difference between the mindset of those that are successful versus those that are unsuccessful. Successful people see value in setbacks while unsuccessful people feel guilty and dwell on failures, which hinder their ability to move forward effectively.

"The saying 'paying your tuition' is terrific. I've never heard that before but I plan on using it in the future," I replied.

"I wish I could take credit for it. However, it was something said to me a long time ago by a very wise family friend. Let me tell you **the story of 'paying your tuition…'**

Many years ago, when I was in my late teens, I was watching an old family friend make glass products in his barn. He was retired, but because he always had a burning desire to create different types of glassware, he decided to start a small glassware company. At first it was a hobby to keep him busy. But after several years, he became an expert and his glassware products were sought after by everyone in our town and the neighboring towns as well.

As I was watching him make a beautiful glass vase for a customer, I asked him how long it took him to produce one. He responded that it took about six hours total. I then asked how many glass vases he had to produce before he mastered this art and produced a vase worthy of selling. He said it took him about **four hundred attempts** before he was satisfied with the quality of the vase. Four hundred attempts at six hours a piece was 2,400 hours. That's roughly more than a year, assuming an eight hour day, five days a week. 'That's a lot of failures and a whole lot of money spent on wasted materials,' I replied to him.

His response; 'Son, it's the tuition I had to pay in order to master my craft and produce a vase I would be proud to sell to a paying customer. Without the dedication, time and money investment, I would not have had a three month backlog of orders waiting to be filled.' It was a lesson I'll never forget."

"This is a great story of how to use failures as another way to learning something new," I replied. "He could have quit after any one of the four hundred failures and would have never mastered his craft."

"Now you see why the majority of people never achieve their desired purposes in life," Abe stated. "It's so easy to just stop and give up. But if you're tenacious and have a dogged determination to achieve, you will succeed."

"Let's now move on to the next much underutilized method of accumulating knowledge and that's **maximizing your time.**" Abe said. **"**Most people will tell you that they can't complete a job, or undertake an additional task, because they don't have the time. That's just plain malarkey! If you add up all the wasted time one spends every day, you'd discover hours of unused, unproductive time!

Let me give you a great example; look at the time you spend traveling to and from work every day. For most people, it's significant. When I first started my career, I use to ride the subway to and from work, which amounted to around two hours a day. So, I made sure to maximize my time by reading something for those two hours every day. I would bring a book, read the business section of the paper, or maybe an article from a trade journal. I would maximize my time to the fullest extent. You mentioned to me that it takes you about three hours to arrive here from your home and then another three hours going back. How do you spend those six hours?"

"Not productively," I replied. "I was just thinking of that exact scenario as you were telling me about the hours you spent reading on the subway. I usually have the radio on, listening to music, switching from station to station. Although part of the ride home is used productively thinking about our lesson."

"Yes, the time spent thinking is time well spent," Abe added, "but unless you're thinking for the entire six hours, why not insert a CD of a book that will provide you knowledge in your pursuit of your defined purposes? You have the advantage of many more options than I had fifty years ago."

"Good idea, Abe. In fact, I spend at least two hours a day commuting in my car, and I always saw it as wasted time. However, if I'm acquiring new knowledge that will help me to succeed, it's no longer wasted time."

"That's correct, Abe replied. And, you'll find you won't be aggravated with the traffic like most others because you're maximizing your time." Next Abe went on to talk about **education and investing in you**.

"I can't begin *to tell you* how many people hesitate to spend money on educating themselves. There is no greater investment then investing in you. Focused education should be considered a necessary investment and not perceived as an additional expense item on your company's or personal income statement. Most people, especially business owners, don't acquire the success they desire because they see education as just an additional cost as opposed to a critical and worthwhile investment."

"What do you mean by *focused education*?" I asked.

"Education that is focused on accumulating as much information, facts, and knowledge as possible towards the achievement of your defined purpose," Abe responded. "Creating your defined purpose- along with your roadmap or blueprint- will allow you to target the knowledge required to help complete the action steps on your blueprint. Without a purpose, without a roadmap, knowing what you need to learn becomes a moving target. This is both inefficient and highly ineffective. Let me provide you with some examples of sound educational investments…"

a) Continuing education courses
b) Educational trainings and conferences
c) Products such as CDs and books
d) Retreats
e) Mentors and coaches
f) Attainment of certifications

"Educate and stimulate young man! Stimulate and feed your mind!"

"These are great examples Abe. When you refer to mentors and coaches, are you referring to establishing a relationship similar to the one we have?"

"I'm glad you asked me that because that leads me into our next approach to accumulating wisdom," Abe replied.

"The answer to your question is partly, yes. You always want to surround yourself with successful and productive people AND **find someone who has already accomplished what you want to accomplish!** They have already made the mistakes and experienced the process of 'paying their tuition.' This experience can provide you with the ultimate shortcut. But most people don't have the opportunity afforded you, young man, so it may be necessary to hire a mentor, or coach, to assist them. A successful and experienced mentor or coach [versed in one's particular industry is invaluable] and should pay for itself immediately."

"I understand and I hope to be in the position one day to pass these same lessons onto others so they can experience an opportunity like I am."

"One day soon, you will! And lastly- we went over this last way to accumulate knowledge in our fifth lesson, and that is **be curious**. Remember, discovery is a matter of investigation, so use your sense of curiosity wherever possible."

Abe's Prosperity Retreat

"Alright, here's the moment you've anxiously been awaiting! I'm now going to show you how to run, what I consider to be, one of the most important and effective strategies directly responsible for me and the other participating members to attain incredible success and prosperity, **'The Prosperity Retreat.'**

If you recall from our third lesson, 'The Prosperity Retreat' was a quarterly retreat comprised of ten targeted, handpicked CEOs, exclusive to their industry. Four times a year, we would travel to a remote and secluded cabin in upstate New York and spend a weekend discussing issues, topics and concepts, and then devising solutions in a coordinated cooperative effort all with the purpose to help each other achieve our defined purposes. As the group's founder, I facilitated our retreats in a very structured and organized way keeping us on track so that each member was given the full attention of all the other members.

'The Prosperity Retreat' was founded on **7 Absolute Principles** that were adhered to at all times. They are as follows:

The 7 Prosperity Retreat Principles

1. **Harmony**-There must be harmonious unification between all members. Any member, who cannot adhere to this rule, will not be asked back to the quarterly retreat.

2. **Confidentiality**-All members must agree to the strictest confidentiality of information discussed by any participant.

3. **Exclusivity**-There can only be one person representing a particular industry in the group as this

prevents members from withholding important information from a perceived competitor.

4. **Participation**-Each member must give their best effort to participate to help the other members achieve their defined purposes. Full participation creates stronger long-term alliances leading to increased coordinated cooperative efforts among group members.

5. **Attention**- Each member agrees to shut off any and all communication devices unless the device is used to take notes. If a cell phone needs to be used to make an emergency call, the member will politely remove themselves from the group session and return when the call is completed. [This principle has been updated for todays' technology.]

6. **Promptness**- All group members agree to be on time for each session so that everyone is in attendance to participate.

7. **Commitment-**All group members will commit to 4 quarterly retreats per year. At the end of each year, each member will let the facilitator know if they plan on committing to participate in the following year.

How The Prosperity Retreat Operates

This is where the conversation got really interesting. After reviewing the principles in detail, Abe reached into the bottom drawer of his desk and pulled out a big three ring binder notebook entitled *The Prosperity Retreat Book #1*. He explained how this was the first of ten different binders all pertaining to the retreats. The first notebook was geared only towards the operations and principles of the retreat whereas the remaining nine binders were detailed notes, compiled by Abe, from each of the retreats, organized by date.

We then spent the next hour reviewing how Abe facilitated and operated the three day weekend. Below summarizes the very first *Prosperity Retreat* held:

Day 1:

7:30-8:00: A light breakfast

8:00-8:15: Opening notes and welcome by Abe

8:15-9:00: Purpose of *The Prosperity Retreat* and review of principles

9:00-12:00: Each member is provided 15 minutes to introduce themselves, explain what type of business they operate as CEO and what they hoped to accomplish from the retreat including their defined purposes and expectations.

As facilitator, Abe would write each participants information with their goals and expectations on a large white sheet of paper and tape it to the wall.

12:00-1:00: A light lunch

1:00-5:00 The group session begins starting with the first participant, randomly chosen by Abe. They circle back to that person's defined purpose and the group spends 1 hour assisting that participant through a process of coordinated cooperative effort. The goal is for that participant to have action steps and solutions to their defined purpose and any issues they are experiencing. Three more participants followed to complete the 1st day.

Again, as facilitator, Abe writes the defined purpose and what that participant wanted to accomplish along with the groups recommended actions steps and solutions on a large white sheet of paper, which is taped to the wall.

6:00- 8:00: Dinner with all participants

Day 2:

7:30-8:00: A light breakfast

8:00-12:00: 4 more participants received their 1 hour each.

12:00-1:00: A light lunch

1:00-3:00: The last 2 participants received their 1 hour with Abe as the final participant.

3:00-5:00: Discussing common issues, topics and solutions amongst all the groups' members. The topics and issues were set forth by Abe.

Day 3:

7:30-8:00: A light Breakfast

8:00-12:00: All group members spent the remaining time discussing the formulation of ongoing strategic organized alliances outside of The Prosperity Retreat.

"Abe, you certainly didn't disappoint. I'm going to start my own prosperity retreats, albeit a modified version locally, to take advantage of the power of organized alliances."

"That's exactly what I was going to suggest to you", Abe replied. "For your assignment, I would like you to revisit the list of people you know that you believe would make a terrific alliance from last month's assignment. Then choose the business owners from that list you would like to join you in a quarterly retreat. Meet with each one individually to explain the goals of the prosperity retreats and invite them to participate."

Then Abe reached back into the bottom drawer of his desk and pulled out another notebook binder with my name on it.

"I've made a copy of my notebook containing the operations and principles of the prosperity retreat along with notes of all the issues, topics and lessons I created. Please do not lose this as this is the only copy I've ever made for anyone. It does not contain any personal information on the members as that is confidential. However, you can use this to facilitate your own prosperity retreats in the future."

"Abe, I'm honored. Thank you so much."

"My pleasure. Have a safe trip back and I'll see you next month!"

I've utilized Abe's prosperity retreats personally for many years. Every member who has participated with me in my group attributes much of their incredible success and prosperity to these retreats. They're now also available to the public through our company where we organize groups of 8 to 10 CEO's exclusive to their industry and are facilitated by me in different beautiful remote areas of the country. You can access more information on the availability of future retreats on www.markluterman.com.)

The Assignment

Read the summary below for today's lesson for how we learn. List the action steps necessary to achieve each one.

1) Make a list of some of the valuable lessons you've learned by experience

2) Make a list of ways you can maximize your time

3) Think of ways to investing in continuing education

4) Find someone who has already accomplished what you want to accomplish and learn what you can from them

5) Keep thinking of ways to keep your curiosity alive

6) Participate in a Prosperity Retreat

Symphony No.8
Play Big

"Leave a lasting legacy for generations to remember."

Upon my eighth visit to Abe, he remarked right away that my demeanor was different.

"Good morning, young man. You seem awfully chipper this morning!" he remarked.

"I am, Abe. Immediately upon my return to Baltimore, I selected seven business owners to join me in a quarterly prosperity retreat. Of the seven, six accepted with enthusiasm, so now I am the proud originator and facilitator of a new, exciting prosperity group!"

"Great news!" Abe exclaimed. "Please keep me informed about your retreats and make sure you use the information I provided you to assist you in operating an efficient and effective retreat. And if you have any questions along the way, don't hesitate to ask…"

"Thanks. I won't."

"OK, so let's move on to today's lesson. I refer to today's lesson as 'Playing Big.' I want you to live your life, and hopefully it's a long, healthy and prosperous one, so that you can **leave a lasting legacy for generations to remember**. I want you to be able to leave a legacy which will outlive you. By having this mindset, you will never settle for mediocrity, which is how the majority of people live their life.

Let me take it one step further. I believe it is your duty, obligation and privilege *not to play 'small'* …dream BIG and then act on it! You only live once! Your time is finite, which no one can ever predict. So use that time wisely and create a lasting legacy. We've all been blessed with the ability to think, the one asset that only you control and no one can take that away from you. And when you possess the ability to think, you have everything you need to create endless opportunities and unlimited success, in perpetuity. You're not limited by anything but yourself.

When you combine your ability to think with a definiteness of purpose, an action plan suited to attain your purpose, take the right action in the present, with an unwavering desire and commitment and an unrelenting faith that you will succeed at all costs, you have the recipe for success, a recipe to leave a lasting legacy for generations to remember."

The Vast Majority

"Young man, the majority of people in this world, who I also refer to as 'the masses,' wander aimlessly through life without any direction or purpose. They play it safe; not wanting to upset the 'apple cart.' They're in their comfort zone with no major decisions to make, never really happy or satisfied, but content just to coast through life. And if there is a major decision to be made, procrastination becomes the dominant thought causing that person to be indecisive."

"Why is that? Why would most people be content to coast through life and not strive for greatness? It makes no sense to me."

"Go back to our lesson on courage. What's the number one reason why people procrastinate and never achieve the success they desire?"

"Abe, I believe it is because of fear. They're afraid."

"And what do they fear?" Abe asked.

"They fear making mistakes and the uncertainty of the future," I replied.

"Yes, that's correct. If they change their behavior, which has been cultivated over the years, it creates too much uncertainty and fear of making a mistake. So, they do *nothing*; procrastinating through life until their life passes them by."

"What can someone do to change this behavior?" I asked.

"Well, the first change occurs because of urgency, not desire. This happens during periods of turmoil or adversity when the only option is to take action such as the loss of employment. One is forced to take action because they have no choice. The second change occurs by creating a defined purpose, a blueprint to achieve this defined purpose followed by taking the right action in the present backed by desire and faith. It's the steps we discussed in our very first lesson. When you play BIG, I want you always to remember:

- Never be fearful of big undertakings.
- Attack your defined purpose with every ounce of energy and vigor you can muster.
- Expect great things from yourself.
- Aim so high that even if you fall a bit short, you will still have accomplished a lot.

The Value of Aiming High

"Imagine for a moment a defined purpose based around one's business, which generates $5 million in revenue and $500,000 in net profits within three years. At the time you create your defined purpose, your company is generating $1 million in revenue and $100,000 in profits. It's an aggressive and ambitious goal, but one you will attack with courage and enthusiasm. Now, let's fast forward three years and the business achieves $4,000,000 in revenue and $400,000 in profits, a terrific rate of growth. Because you've dreamed big and attacked your defined purpose with courage, you've created a very healthy company, primed for a great future, even if you've fallen a bit short of your ambitious goal.

This applies to any defined purpose. Take for example an employee starting out as a commissioned salesperson. Their defined purpose may be to become Vice President of the entire sales division in five years. So- fast forward five years later and this employee is in charge of all National Accounts with a sales force of ten people working under them. Although, they've yet to achieve their ultimate ambitious goal, they've still managed to create a great deal of success within their desired timeframe."

"Abe, this makes sense a lot of sense. However, when can one be too ambitious, or unrealistic, in their defined purpose?"

"That's a great question," Abe replied. "Remember that in order to achieve your defined purpose you must have an unrelenting faith and belief that you will be successful. So, whatever you're purpose, make sure you truly believe it can be attained because there are no limitations. Nature has provided us with an abundance of resources available to everyone. This is called the *Principle of Abundant and Plentiful Resources.*"

The Principle of Abundant and Plentiful Resources

"Under this principle, all resources, possessions and material objects we desire are already in existence in abundance, enough for everyone to share. All that's required is for the rightful owner to claim them."

"What is a 'rightful owner,' I asked?"

"A rightful owner is one whose undivided attention is focused on attaining these resources through their defined purpose, backed by action steps which are productive and never cause harm to anyone," Abe answered. "A rightful owner must also have the mindset of abundancy. They must think abundance, see abundance, feel abundance, and believe in abundance. Limitations of any sort can never be present. This principle is available to *everyone,* without constraints or limitations. It only discriminates against those who wander aimlessly through life without any direction or purpose. Now, for your assignment..."

The Assignment

**A Summary
of The Principle of Abundance**

1. Revisit your success statement. Are you 'playing big' with your defined purpose? Will it leave a lasting legacy? Keep in mind, the engine behind it is **passion!**
2. Refresh yourself on the lyrics of Playing BIG below:

✓ All resources, possessions and material objects we desire are already in existence.

✓ All resources, possessions and material objects are abundant and plentiful.

✓ All resources, possessions and material objects are waiting to be claimed by its rightful owner.

✓ Any need we have can be met with the right mindset and thoughts. You must think abundance, see abundance, feel abundance, and believe abundance.

✓ Limitations of any sort can never be present. Self-doubt cannot exist.

✓ Everyone can participate.

Symphony No. 9
The Ballad of Life

"You Must Enrich the Lives of Others In Order to
Attain the Riches and Successes You Desire."

As I drove north once again towards New York City, I realized that is was just eight months ago that I had created a success statement that I felt was challenging. But after our session on 'Play BIG,' I had a completely different perspective. It was centered around my company and personal success, but certainly did not include a lasting legacy for generations to come.

For several weeks, I felt perplexed. *What would I love to do, backed by incredible passion that would leave a lasting legacy for generations to remember?* I asked myself that question, over and over, hoping the power of self-suggestion would kick in. Sure enough, as I was driving home one evening a week before this session, it hit me like a ton of bricks; an idea that inspired me to play big and leave a lasting legacy. As soon as I arrived home, I created an additional success statement centered around this new and exciting idea. I was now ready to share it with Abe, hoping he would find it an acceptable and worthwhile endeavor.

As I walked through his door, there he was.

"Good morning, Abe!" I said, hardly able to contain my excitement.

"Good morning, young man. I was just finishing my preparation for today's lesson. I've been away for a good part of the month so I fell a bit behind. I'm very excited for today's lesson. Use this lesson consistently and properly, and you will achieve greatness. But before we begin, you had an assignment to revisit your success statement...What did you discover?"

"Abe, this was tough, but enlightening. I formed a completely different angle on my success statement after last month's lesson. I no longer felt like my defined purpose would allow me to leave a lasting legacy. It would create personal and financial success, but not something for perpetuity. So, I created an additional plan that coincides with a bigger dream. It wasn't easy. It took several weeks of persistent thought. Then, driving home one evening, the idea just came to me!"

"Do tell..."

"Well, here it is...I'm a bit hesitant to share because it involves you..."

"Don't be hesitant. Please share, young man."

"OK, Abe. At the appropriate time, after I've achieved my personal and financial goals relating to my company, I would like to share *your lessons*, the lessons you're teaching me right now- your life's work, your successes, and the wisdom you've developed- with people all around the world. I want everyone who is open to this wisdom to be able to have access to it.

I'd like to refer to these lessons as '*Symphonies*,' passed on from a teacher to his student. I will travel the world espousing these symphonies to help people create unlimited success. This will be communicated by telling the story of our journey together. I am passionate about this, but will only pursue it with your blessing."

"Young man, I don't know what to say. I'm truly honored and proud of you. What an incredible idea. You have my blessing and my complete support!"

"Abe, I do recognize however that I must use these lessons personally and create my own life experiences and successes before I feel justified in presenting them to others. So, this is not something that will happen overnight. It will be years before I feel comfortable presenting this information to others."

"You'll know when the time is right," Abe replied. "The best part of this purpose is your commitment to helping others. I told you months ago how I don't believe in coincidences. I believe everything happens for a reason. Today is another great example."

"How's that?"

"Mark, your purpose of helping others, which you shared with me today as your defined purpose, is the topic of today's lesson. I refer to it as enriching the lives of others. It's like 'the ballad of life,' that's sung over and over again, until it reaches many lives. This is part of the success you desire."

The Parable of The Spoons

"Young man, do you know what a parable is?"

"Sure- it's a story which teaches a point or a lesson."

"Right. The story I want to share with you today is called *The Parable of Spoons*. Once, there was a holy man who was having a conversation with the Lord, who said, 'Lord, I would like to know what Heaven and Hell are like.' The Lord led the holy man to two doors. He opened one of the doors and the holy man looked in. In the middle of the room was a large round table. In the middle of the table was a large pot of stew which smelled delicious and made the holy man's mouth water.

The people sitting around the table were thin and sickly. They appeared to be famished. They were holding spoons with very long handles and they were able to reach into the pot of stew and take a spoonful but, because the handle was longer than their arms, they could not get the spoons back into their mouths. The holy man shuddered at the sight of their misery and suffering. The Lord said, 'You have seen Hell.'

They went to the next room and opened the door. It was exactly the same as the first one. There was the large round table with the large pot of stew which made the holy man's mouth water. The people were equipped with the same long-handled spoons, but here the people were well nourished and plump, laughing and talking. The holy man said, 'I don't understand?'

'It is simple,' said the Lord, 'It requires but one skill. You see, they have learned to feed each other. While the greedy think only of themselves.'

So- look to help others at every opportunity possible and embrace generosity, kindness and the habit of serving others. It is the quickest way to achieving success and happiness. Everything that we receive comes to us from serving others."

"Abe, I don't believe I'm greedy but I do get consumed in my own thoughts and at times, thinking only of myself and about my problems and concerns."

"Most people do. They become so entrenched in their own lives, their own little worries, fears, conflicts and predicaments that everything else around them is inconsequential. They become lost in their own world believing their problems and issues are more difficult than everyone else. However, there's nothing like getting outside your own 'bubble' to enrich lives of others and –in turn- enrich yours. The worth you create is immeasurable _monetarily_. I believe enriching others' lives also heals one's soul, gives your life new meaning and with it brings peace of mind. Look- if you took all of your problems, worries and fears and set them next to most people, you'd find your life is pretty darn good."

"You're right; I never looked at it that way."

"But unfortunately, that's the mindset of the majority of people in our universe," Abe added. "It's also a key reason why most business owners ultimately fail."

The Ultimate Question

"Over the course of my life, I've probably spoken to several hundred business organizations on various topics. At the beginning of each presentation, I always asked the same question, 'Why are you in business?' Do you know what the overwhelming response was?"

"Probably to make money or take care of their family," I guessed.

"That's right ...and it is absolutely the wrong outlook for one to be successful. You are in business to serve your customers and provide a benefit that will produce tremendous value. Always **over–deliver** for your customers, give them more than what they expect, and you'll be rewarded with a disproportionate share of additional business. The more service you provide, the greater the reward. You should always be asking the questions:

1) How does this benefit my customer?
2) How much value will my customer receive?
3) How have I /we provided an enriching experience?

As opposed to:
1) How does this benefit me?
2) How much money will this make me?
3) How will this experience enrich my life?

This mindset is the only way to cultivate success in perpetuity. But this mindset should not be limited to those in business. Every person should seek to enrich the lives of others. When one engages in this mindset, they are accessing from nature *The Law of Unlimited and Infinite Returns.*"

The Law of Unlimited and Infinite Returns

"The Law of Unlimited and Infinite Returns happens when you render incredible service and value. In return, you are rewarded far more than the service and value you rendered. This also works in reverse. If you choose to harm or take advantage of another, you will be penalized in the future for these adverse actions. You may be aware of this occurrence by the term *karma.*"

"I am familiar with that term, Abe."

"Young man, the universe will return to you exactly what you deserve. Give more than you receive and you will access the positive power of nature and will be rewarded for your actions. But, make sure you enrich the lives of others because **you want to** and not because you expect something in return. There can never be any ulterior motives. Your only expectation should be the wonderful feeling you receive from providing value and benefit to another person. Whatever reward nature provides you is a bonus.

If you are willing to assist others before trying to accumulate riches for the betterment of yourself, there is a world full of abundant opportunities waiting for you. So for your assignment, I would like you to awaken each day with the conviction of enriching the lives of at least three people for the day. Then, I want you to act on this conviction. Record each action along with the feeling you receive in return. Remember, even the simplest actions have merit."

"This is an exciting assignment, Abe. I've never truly recognized the importance of helping and assisting others. But will I be able to find three actions every day?"

"You will. You'll be presented with so many opportunities to help people, you'll lose count. Opportunities for providing value, benefits, kindness and generosity are in endless supply if you utilize one of our previous lessons, being aware of your surroundings. Also, remember what I said regarding the simplest actions having merit, such as holding the door open for another or allowing a vehicle to merge in front of you. These acts of enrichment count just the same.

Before we conclude today's lesson, I want to explain the importance of *thought*. Thoughts are essential as they form the basis of habit through the power of self-suggestion. Self-suggestion is a communication link between the conscious and sub-conscious minds. The dominate thoughts of the conscious mind reach the subconscious mind and influence it, whether they are positive or negative. Your subconscious mind nurtured by these thoughts will then act upon them and supply you with ideas and plans to help you achieve whatever it is you desire. I want you to utilize the power of self-suggestion to form the habit of enrichment as part of your everyday protocol. Upon receiving the idea or plan to help another, act on it. Does that make sense?"

"It does, Abe!"

"Great. I look forward to the completion of your assignment. Have a great month!"

"You too, Abe!"

The Assignment

1) Awaken each day with the conviction of enriching the lives of at least three people for the day. Then, act on this conviction. Record each action along with the feeling you receive in return. Remember, even the simplest actions have merit.

2) Review the below summary:

A Summary of the Law of Unlimited and Infinite Returns

✓ Render incredible service with boundless benefits and value and you will be rewarded far more than the service you rendered.

✓ Give more than you receive.

✓ When you give; give because you want to and not because you expect something in return.

✓ If you are willing to assist others before trying to accumulate riches for the betterment of yourself, there is a world full of abundant opportunities waiting for you.

Symphony No.10

A Song of Grace

"Grace is forgiveness without requiring the other person to ask."

The preparation for this session began the minute I left Abe's apartment and began driving back to Baltimore. Remembering that the principle of enrichment begins with the actual thought, I spent three hours in the car thinking of ways I could help people. Through this process, I began creating ideas and concepts I hadn't thought of before. By the time I reached our next session...

"Good morning, young man. I hope the past several weeks have brought you an abundance of happiness and joy."

"They have, Abe. Enriching the lives of others is now part of my daily protocol. I awake each day with thoughts on how I could improve the lives of at least three people, and after about the third week, it became instinctive. What I discovered is there is an endless, infinite list of actions you can provide to others to help enrich their lives. For example, I found myself holding doors open for people, saying 'bless you' to people who sneezed, smiling and saying hello to individuals who I'd never met before, telling the cashier at the grocery store to have a blessed day, giving money to people who were homeless, [no act too small], volunteering for philanthropic tasks, and the list went on.

I began a journal, which recorded each act and the corresponding feeling I received. You'll see from my documentation of my feelings [I handed Abe my journal] that every act brought me happiness and joy; even the simplest and smallest acts."

"This is wonderful," he said after taking fifteen minutes to review my journal. "You've served yourself and others with great distinction and I can see these acts were completed without expecting anything in return. Well done."

"Thanks, Abe!"

"Now… let's get started on today's lesson, which is instrumental towards your future success and happiness: forgiveness. Forgiveness is a very important, yet highly underutilized attribute which all successful people possess. Most often, forgiveness is left out of the success equation. But the truth is, when you hold grudges against others, when you dwell in the past, or when you are consumed with bitterness, anger and resentment, you harness negative energy. This will impact your ability to think and focus on achieving whatever it is you desire.

Please remember this from today's lesson: **Nothing is more draining or debilitating than harnessing negative energy.** You must release it. Holding on to it only hurts *you*. When you are able to forgive, you release the negative energy that keeps you from thinking positive thoughts. It's these positive thoughts that directly impact your ability to think and develop constructive and creative ideas, enabling you to move forward with your ultimate goal of achieving your defined purpose. Forgiveness should also be voluntary and without conditions. True grace is forgiveness without requiring the other person to ask."

"Abe, how do you turn off the hurt and anger you feel when someone has intentionally tried to hurt you?"

Abe's Experience with Forgiveness

"That's a great question and one I can't answer without sharing with you my past experiences with anger and resentment…When I was younger, my behavior was predictable. My temper was short and I would lash out at the slightest provocation, especially if I felt someone was attempting to take advantage of me, or harm me, in any way. Not only would I lash out, I then held a grudge in perpetuity. If I saw this person at an event or in public, I would ignore them and walk by as if they didn't exist.

But it wouldn't stop there. Even though I wouldn't acknowledge their existence I would ruminate about them and their actions, over and over in my mind; concoct stories of revenge and retaliation. Of course, I would never act on it, but the thoughts would consume me. Little did I know how dangerous those thoughts were. They were draining my energy and hindering my ability to concentrate and focus on my goals and ambitions. I was allowing the past to affect the present as well as my future.

And, it was affecting my relationships with my family and friends. I would find myself developing mood swings caused by these debilitating thoughts. I would be present physically, but mentally, I was somewhere else. This was very frustrating to my family, especially my wife.

I can remember one example where I was in the middle of selling one of our companies. The buyer and his team of attorneys demonstrated every intention of going through with the purchase. But the negotiations seemed to drag on inexplicably for months, the terms of the deal becoming more unreasonable by the minute. Finally, I realized there was no intention to buy the company. Their goal was to learn as much information about our business so they could start their own division. I became outraged, berated the buyer and his team of lawyers and fumed for nearly a month. My curtness, impatience and negative energy was very frustrating and challenging to those who were close to me. And this was just one of many examples occurring over a period of prosperous, yet unenjoyable years."

"What did you do? How did you change?" I asked.

"The first step was recognition. Remember our lesson on accountability?"

"Absolutely," I replied.

"I recognized how my thoughts were directly responsible for impairing my better judgement and causing me to create unnecessary negativity in my life. Then I began reading about the mind and how powerful our thoughts are, especially negative thoughts. You see, a simple thought triggers an emotion. In other words, if you are conceiving an imaginary negative event, you'll trigger a negative emotion such as anger, frustration, hatred, anxiety and depression. And then it hit me. The only one I was harming with these adversarial thoughts was *me*. So I immediately set out to change the one thing I can control, my own thoughts.

So let's go back to the example I just shared with you. First, I had no control over the other parties' actions. However, I could control my own *reaction*. Here are three possible reactions:

a) Negatively, and retaliate in anger and spite in order to harm the other party.

b) Negatively, not retaliate but remain angry, frustrated and hold onto vicious thoughts, hoping that something negative happens to the other party OR…

c) Positively, and recognize the event as an opportunity to learn something new.

Fortunately, I was smart enough to avoid option A. Unfortunately, I opted for option B and allowed this incident to negatively impact me for a substantial period of time."

"If you opted for C, what would you have learned?" I asked.

"Great question, as usual. Here's what option C would teach…"

1) How to tell a serious buyer from one looking to extract information; preventing this from occurring again.
2) That losing my temper showed weakness and a lack of leadership.
3) The only person harmed by my anger and frustration is me, and those close to me.
4) Harnessing negative energy creates stagnation and pulls your focus from taking right action in the present.
5) I can only control my reactions, not the actions of anyone else.
6) Showing grace is much better than holding on to anger.
7) Know that when someone wrongs you, it's all about the other person's insecurities and their lack of character.
8) Total emotional freedom is necessary to achieve whatever success you desire.

"So you can take any event and turn a negative experience into a positive outcome just with your thought process, the right mindset?" I asked.

"That's absolutely correct," Abe responded. "This is one of the hidden secrets of being successful. Success depends on your ability to see through adversity and misfortune by remaining focused on your defined purpose without falling victim to negative emotions, which only serve to trigger negative outcomes. The majority of people in this world never learn this lesson. They proceed through life holding grudges against those who have wronged them and carry those grudges to their grave. Think about the amount of time they wasted holding onto this negative energy and what could've been accomplished if they would have used their time more effectively."

"I know many people who do this, Abe. However, when someone intentionally attempts to harm you in business, or otherwise, doesn't it bother you when there's no consequences for their actions?"

"But there **are** consequences, young man. Every action has a consequence; good or bad. Remember from our previous lesson of enriching the lives of others? The universe will return to you exactly what you've created. A person who lies, cheats or steals may elude negative repercussions at that moment, but eventually their dishonest ways will be dealt with accordingly. So forgive and allow nature to handle the rest. Here are three important steps to forgiveness…"

Three Steps to Forgiveness

a) Forgive those who have wronged you unconditionally remembering that true grace is forgiveness without requiring the other person to ask.

b) To forget. Many people forgive, but they can't forget. One cannot work without the other. In order to accomplish total emotional freedom, you need both.

c) Forgive yourself. Everyone makes mistakes. Unfortunately, most people are consumed with guilt and shame, two self-inflicted emotions which impede our ability to successfully move forward in life. Learn from mistakes and then immediately move on. A setback is only permanent if you *allow it*. You, as much as anyone else, deserve forgiveness.

"I'm glad you mentioned the third step, Abe, because at times, I am consumed with guilt over past experiences, which I wish I could take back. Maybe I said something I shouldn't have, or wasn't forthcoming with the truth or didn't treat someone with the proper respect. I wrestle with forgiving myself."

"And most people do," replied Abe, "but you must remember **that person** is not the guy I see before me now. You've grown, evolved, and learned from those past experiences to mold you into the person you are today. For that- you should be grateful. Unfortunately, no one has a plane ticket back to the past, so you can't go back. Feeling guilty only serves to keep you *in the past,* reliving old negative experiences which anchors you, keeping you from moving forward. Release negative energy, forgive yourself and feel good about the person you are *today*. You deserve it. You deserve happiness and all the successes in the world!"

"Thanks, Abe!"

"Before we conclude today's lesson, I want to read you a wonderful poem, *The Children's Song* by the famous poet

Rudyard Kipling. The next to last verse reads so eloquently with a reference to forgiveness."

The Children's Song

Land of our Birth, we pledge to thee
Our love and toil in the years to be;
When we are grown and take our place
As men and women with our race.

Father in Heaven who lovest all,
Oh, help Thy children when they call;
That they may build from age to age
An undefiled heritage.

Teach us to bear the yoke in youth,
With steadfastness and careful truth;
That, in our time, Thy Grace may give
The Truth whereby the Nations live.

Teach us to rule ourselves alway,
Controlled and cleanly night and day;
That we may bring, if need arise,
No maimed or worthless sacrifice.

Teach us to look in all our ends
On Thee for judge, and not our friends;
That we, with Thee, may walk uncowed
By fear or favour of the crowd.

Teach us the Strength that cannot seek,
By deed or thought, to hurt the weak;
That, under Thee, we may possess
Man's strength to comfort man's distress.

Teach us Delight in simple things,
And Mirth that has no bitter springs;
Forgiveness free of evil done,
And Love to all men 'neath the sun!

Land of our Birth, our faith, our pride,
For whose dear sake our fathers died;
Oh, Motherland, we pledge to thee
Head, heart and hand through the years to be!

"Now, for your assignment…"

The Assignment

1) Make a list of all the people who have wronged you in the past. Then visualize forgiving them; see yourself shaking their hand, smiling and saying the words: '*I forgive you for your past indiscretions towards me.*'

2) List the actions and then the emotion that was evoked in each instance of you feeling 'wronged.' Explore that emotion and write down how you would have handled it differently, or better. Then, write the following sentence next to it: *I forgive myself and am grateful for the lesson I've learned allowing me to grow and evolve into the person I am today.*"

Symphony No.II

A Grateful Voice

*"People are attracted to kindness and being acknowledged.
It makes them feel important."*

Even as I drove home, I had already started visualizing shaking the hands and smiling to all the people who I felt had 'wronged' me in the past. I saw myself saying the words, *'I forgive you for your past indiscretions towards me.'* Additionally, I also began forgiving myself. Whenever I would feel guilty, I listed the cause of this guilt and wrote the following sentence next to it: *I forgive myself and am grateful for the lesson I've learned allowing me to grow and evolve into the person I am today.*

This exercise really worked. I began to feel liberated with more energy, less clutter in my mind and a renewed focus on the things that were important to me and my family.

As I entered the apartment on our eleventh meeting, I was feeling particularly liberated and I imparted this to Abe after our normal greetings. I expanded on my 'ah-ha' moments; that I had expended way too much energy on revenge and that this habit had been draining me, adversely affecting my attitude and behavior towards others. Replacing this mindset with one of forgiveness was directly responsible for this invigorating feeling. It was as if a weight which had been lifted off my shoulders. Abe just listened and grinned, nodded his head occasionally. I knew he understood. Then we launched into the lesson.

"Well, this lesson should help to accelerate this new energetic state of mind, young man. It's all about the 'Power of Gratitude.' Gratitude is an essential characteristic you should use in all facets of your life. People are attracted to kindness and have an intense desire to be acknowledged. It gives people one of the human needs: significance. It makes them feel appreciated and when people feel appreciated, they respond in kind. This works across every facet of life, so let's begin..."

The Voice of Gratitude

"In business, I firmly believe the 'Power of Gratitude' is the most effective business strategy for growing your company. It creates a herd of loyal, long-term customers who continually purchase your services and products; year after year after year. In addition to purchasing your products and services, your customers become ambassadors and cheerleaders for your company. You create such a memorable experience for them, they can't wait to tell others. Your customers become walking billboards. This, of course, leads to referrals, which is the most efficient and effective way to build a highly profitable enterprise.

The power of gratitude should be applied by all members of the company; from the owner to the sales team to customer service representatives, anyone who has communication with your customers. This may sound simplistic, but most organizations simply choose to ignore it. They take their customers for granted creating a culture of entitlement and a lack of appreciation. But when the foundation of your company is built on gratitude and kindness you create a model where other companies in your industry are completely irrelevant."

"Abe, when you refer to other companies in an industry, do you mean competition?" I asked.

"Yes," Abe replied, "however, I don't like the term *competition* [because the only competition you have is yourself]. You can throw away that term because if you implement and execute the right values, philosophies, and principles throughout your entire organization, you won't have to worry about 'competition.' Price elasticity becomes irrelevant as long as your prices are not egregious. If you have to sell on price, you become nothing more than a commodity where the lowest price wins. In essence, the lowest price loses because your profit margins continue to deteriorate until they no longer can support the company's overhead."

"How do you implement this principle? Where do you start and how do you teach this to an entire organization?" I inquired.

The 'Power of Gratitude' for Customers

"Young man, as Ralph Waldo Emerson once said, *'An institution is the lengthened shadow of one man.'* In other words, it starts with **you**; your organization will follow your lead. You begin by implementing systems and strategies based around demonstrating gratitude. And, although the strategies may vary depending on the size of your company, they should be utilized at all times. Here are some examples [both in your personal life and in business] I recommend..."

a) Answering the phone with a welcoming and pleasant voice.

b) Make it easy to reach your company and provide consistent world-class service.

c) When speaking with a current customer, make sure you get their name and then refer to them by their name during your conversation. Treat them as if their part of the company family.

d) When it's a prospective customer, make sure you thank them and show your appreciation for them taking the time to call *your company*, as there are many choices for your customers.

e) Always make sure you've answered your customer's questions to their liking and ask them if there's anything else you can assist them with.

f) Send thank you letters to customers. Handwritten are the most effective.

g) Take care of the 'senders' not just the 'spenders.' Send thank you letters and a gift, when appropriate, to customers who send you referrals.

h) Get to know your customers, their likes and hobbies. Remember the more you know about them, the more important they feel.

i) Make follow-up calls to insure your customers are satisfied with your product or service. If they're not, take the time to find out why, and do everything possible to correct the issue.

j) If you see an article or story relating to a particular customer's interest, cut it out and send it to them accompanied by a handwritten note that you were thinking of them.

k) If you see a customer featured in an article send it to them with a congratulatory note.

l) Send sympathy and condolence cards when learning about a loss or illness.

m) Recognize other special occasions, such as birthdays, by sending a card.

"The list of things you can do to acknowledge and make your customers and prospects feel important is endless!"

Abe shared another tidbit; that most companies fall in love with the chase, meaning they continually chase after new customers but forget to take care of their current customers. Before you pursue more clients fall in love with your current customers first. Cultivate these relationships as much as you can and you will create an army of loyal customers.

"But it doesn't stop with just your customers and prospects!" He added excitedly, "spread your grateful voice liberally, and in every corner of your business…"

The 'Power of Gratitude': Beyond Your Customers

a) Be appreciative of your vendors/suppliers. Thank them for their service, pay them in a timely way, be accessible. If you plan on being late with a payment, communicate that up front. Treat them with respect and recognize their value to the success of your company. In return, they'll be engaged and committed to your company's success.

b) Be gracious when speaking with people at business and networking events. Speak less about yourself and listen more to what their saying. Take a genuine and sincere interest in other people's lives and you'll leave a positive lasting impression that will benefit you in the future.

c) Make it a point to remember people's names. When you refer to a person by name, it illustrates sincerity and respect.

The 'Power of Gratitude' in Your Organization

"Use your grateful voice inside your company or organization. <u>Everyone</u> is important to the success of your company. A happy employee is usually a very productive employee so here are some recommendations…"

a) Always listen to their ideas. Be grateful and appreciative whether you implement them or not.

b) Show gratitude when they successfully complete a task and share their accomplishments with the rest of the organization.

c) Acknowledge their value and contributions to the organization.

d) Plan company gatherings to celebrate joyous occasions.

e) Treat them to lunch from time to time.

f) Listen attentively and show a genuine and sincere interest when they share information about their personal lives, such as their children's achievements.

g) Look for opportunities to enrich their lives. Remember, no act is too small.

h) When mistakes occur, be calm and composed and try to use it as an opportunity to teach/learn something new.

"I made it my policy every morning, young man, to walk through my entire organization and greet every person I saw with 'good morning.' I would also select at least one employee daily and get to know them better. I wanted to insure each person felt a sense of importance and worth to our company. This created a culture and foundation based around appreciation, respect, honesty and accountability and- in turn- our staff worked harder to help attain our defined purposes."

Gratitude for Yourself

"As important as it is to celebrate others, don't forget about <u>yourself</u>. You're important too so celebrate 'wins', both big and small. Acknowledge the skills and attributes you have acquired. Show gratitude for **you** by..."

a) Celebrating your successes by treating yourself to something you enjoy doing.

b) Compliment yourself for all the lives you've enriched and the kind things you've done for others.

c) Set aside '**you**' time; personal and unstructured time to recharge.

d) Look in the mirror and tell yourself how proud you are of your accomplishments.

e) Celebrate what you have and the opportunities you've been blessed with.

"Every day," Abe continued, "I'm grateful and give thanks for my existence, for being alive, for the universe I live in. I'm grateful for all the gifts I've received: my family, friends and all the people I've touched, and who've touched me. I'm grateful for my shortcomings and setbacks, which have provided me the opportunity to learn something new. I treat each moment in life with gratitude and never, ever take for granted all of the wonderful opportunities and blessings I've received."

"Abe, I can see there is real power in gratitude. I am visualizing implementing gratitude in business and in my personal life as you were speaking… However, I must admit, showing gratitude for *myself* will be the most difficult."

"I completely understand," Abe concurred. "I found it difficult as well. I would dwell on past setbacks and never celebrate successes. I took for granted my accomplishments, as if it they were to be expected. Ask yourself this; *Is it fair to omit celebrating your accomplishments and contributions?* Of course not! Happiness and emotional freedom cannot be attained without first acknowledging the journey that accompanies your defined purposes."

"I see your point. I'm going to work on changing my outlook on ME!"

"Your assignment will assist you in new ways to celebrate YOU, " Abe smiled.

"I am curious though Abe. When you say you're grateful and give thanks, to whom are you being thankful?"

"Great question. I'm so glad you asked. It's a subject that's very important to me and one I wanted to cover with you today."

The Power of Prayer

"Young man, do you remember step 5 from our first lesson?'

"Of course… *You must have an unrelenting faith and belief in the process of accomplishing your clear and defined purpose.*"

"That's correct," Abe replied. "For me, I place my faith in a higher being, a supreme-being, God. Prayer is an essential part of my day and I give thanks continually to God for everything he has bestowed upon me. It is the most powerful form of gratitude. My faith, through prayer, provides me the power to be my best at all times. In times of turmoil or confusion, it helps guide me to make difficult decisions."

Abe then reached behind his desk and selected a beautifully bound antique Old Testament bible and laid it upon his desk.

"I read this every night before I go to sleep," he said. Many successful people that I know [and converse with] are people of faith who use prayer to give thanks and guide them on a daily basis."

"Abe, I have a strong belief in God but do not use prayer in my daily activities. I will begin immediately and start by giving thanks and showing gratitude for all the blessings I receive."

"But don't stop there. I also believe in the power of prayer for others," Abe responded." I believe prayer gives strength to others while also lifting their spirits. It is the highest form of enrichment you can bestow to another."

For the next hour Abe shared with me examples of how prayer really helped him get through some tough times. It was very enlightening and I was honored he trusted me enough to share these examples.

"Before you leave, take this with you."

Abe then presented me with an additional bible he had in his library.

"Abe, I'm honored and touched. Thank you so much!"

"You're welcome; have a great month!"

The Assignment

1) Compile a daily list of examples of gratitude in business and in your personal life

2) Create a list of successes [big and small] and how you celebrated them, or will celebrate them.

3) List the qualities and attributes which you like about yourself.

Symphony No.12

March to Your Drummer

"It's not okay to be normal. You must be above normal, which requires independent thinking, creativity and the courage to persevere."

As soon as I got back to work the following Monday, I called a staff meeting to discuss the power of gratitude and how we were going to implement into our culture. Never once did I disclose where I learned this philosophy because aside from my wife, no one knew of my relationship with Abe or my monthly excursions.

The first objective was to teach everyone how to incorporate gratitude with our customers, prospects, vendors and any other business relationships. We arranged a two hour morning meeting each week to work on different aspects of gratitude; things like how to answer the phone, how to provide great service, or acknowledge a job well-done. We spent one meeting discussing how to use gratitude amongst ourselves.

After thirty days, there was noticeable difference in our company's culture. Gratitude became an integral part of how we approached all aspects of our operations, including inter-company relationships. My personal favorite was celebrating our staff. It gave me pleasure to congratulate them on a job well done and to feel their excitement when lunch was provided, or a company event was planned around them. All of these acts, individually and collectively, led to higher productivity and a much more positive working environment.

My grateful voice spilled over into my personal life, as well. I spoke less and listened more. I took a genuine and sincere interest in other people's lives. I recorded these acts of gratitude, both personally and professionally, by date in my diary, per Abe's instructions.

I considered this paradigm shift a great accomplishment and celebrated the success by taking my family to my favorite restaurant and complimenting myself for a job well done. I recorded this in my diary as well as all other personal accomplishments during the month.

Prayer is the most powerful form of gratitude so coming into session twelve I was feeling grateful to Abe for teaching me the importance of giving thanks to my supreme being.

"Good morning, young man," he said with a grin.

"Good morning!"

"So- how was this past month?"

"Full of gratitude, Abe."

He smiled as I shared what I had accomplished around gratitude and how I implemented it in all areas of my life. Then, I handed him the list.

"As usual, a job well done, he replied."

"I must say- it lifted my spirits, and made me feel better about myself. But the most life-altering for me was the power of prayer. During this past month, I prayed and read the Bible (Old Testament) every day. Whenever I felt anxious or stressed, I created the following affirmation, which I repeated continuously; 'I believe God will always help me make the best decision and guide me in the right direction.' Immediately I would feel a sense of tranquility." Abe smiled. He knew exactly the feeling I was describing.

"I'm so happy to hear this. The beauty of prayer is its available anytime, anywhere and in as much quantity as you desire. There's nothing more powerful than prayer and your belief and faith in your supreme being. Shall we begin?"

Independent Thinking

"It's <u>not</u> okay to be normal," Abe began, "You must be *above normal* [or abnormal], which requires independent thinking, creativity and the courage to persevere."

"How do you define being *normal?*"

"Great question. Normal is relying on others to make decisions for you. Normal is not using your own thoughts to succeed. Being normal is one of the most common reasons business owners and people in general fail. They're easily swayed by what the masses do [or don't do] and they may discover that they've been led down, the wrong path, or the path to failure. Remember what we've discussed in previous lessons? The masses, the overwhelming majority, are usually wrong.

Independent thinkers, conversely, are people of courage because they're unafraid to make their own decisions and accept responsibility for the consequences that follow, good or bad. Do you know why independent thinkers are people of courage?"

"I believe so…As you've taught me, when you have courage, you're unafraid to make mistakes because you know failures are nothing more than temporary defeats. Failing is an absolute necessity to being successful. The defeats we encounter are necessary because you learn more about how to succeed from failing than from the so-called successes. So if you know the failures are opportunities to learn something new, then there's really nothing to be fearful of."

"I couldn't have said it better myself," added Abe.

The Most Incredible Gift

"Thinking is the most incredible gift; the ability to contemplate *everything!* With that, you have all the tools to create endless opportunities and unlimited success. Your thoughts are the genesis of where every great discovery starts. Thoughts lead to ideas, then strategies which can become reality.

Your ability to think is controlled only by **you**. So why would anyone want to relinquish control of this incredible power to others? Unfortunately, when you rely on others to make decisions for you, you relinquish that control. Once you relinquish that control, if failure follows, you have no one to blame but yourself."

"Abe, where do you see most people relinquishing control?"

Marching to Another's Drum

"If you recall from our lesson on controlling your environment, when I was in my late twenties, married and with three young children, I wanted to start my own company rather than work for someone else. Aside from my wife, everyone I knew, including my own parents discouraged me from following my dream. Remember how they were telling me to keep the steady salary? And how it was irresponsible of me to put my family at risk?

However, I had a hunch, a premonition that I was heading in the right direction. I listened to my inner thoughts and it was the best business decision I ever made. This is a great example of people relinquishing control. They have an idea, they discuss the idea with others to get their opinions. Frequently, they'll hear every reason why the idea won't work and how they're wasting their time. I refer to these kind of people as 'the masses' or 'naysayers.' Unfortunately, most people will listen to the naysayers and the idea dies before it has a chance to develop into reality."

"So based on this example, is it better to *avoid* asking other people their opinion?" I asked.

"Again, remember the lesson on controlling your environment. Only ask people and allies that create a positive environment, inspire you and are willing to help you achieve your defined purpose," Abe replied. "If you believe strongly in the idea, asking someone's opinion should only be directed to gain insight or knowledge to assist you. It should not be directed to whether you should or shouldn't pursue the idea.

Here's another example…approximately thirty years ago, as part of our portfolio, we owned a large heating and air conditioning company, with multiple locations across the Mid-Atlantic region. As with all of our companies, we meet with the president and his executive team quarterly to review the previous quarter's results of operations. Due to a particularly harsh winter with record snowfalls, the company realized significant losses. There were days when roads were too treacherous for technicians to service customers, and employees didn't show up for work.

When asked about the significant losses, the president blamed the weather and justified how this was acceptable because all the other business owners he spoke to in this region were experiencing poor operating results as well.

The justification was unacceptable as it was the telltale sign of a lack of independent thinking. Relying on what other business owners do, or don't do, is a roadmap to failure. This falls into the 'action vs. reaction' category. I would say that a preemptive plan would have been a good idea."

"Give me an example; what should the president and his executive team have done to prepare for an event out of their control such as a harsh winter?" I asked.

"The company had serviced over ten thousand customers since its inception. The independent thinker would have prepared for this event by forming alliances with other companies who thrive when natural disasters occur such as a snow removal company. The harsh winter didn't occur overnight. Weeks leading up to the record snowfall and cold temperatures, news stations were reporting the strong possibility of a blizzard hitting the Mid-Atlantic region. This provided ample time to form the alliance, how the profits would be split and a mass mailing to the customer base informing them of our newest service and the high likelihood of a major blizzard.

Furthermore, the slowdown also provided an opportunity for our executive team to use the time to review our existing customer list and call any customers who currently were not covered under our annual preventive maintenance plan; a highly profitable recurring revenue source. The calls could have been made from their homes if they were unable to drive to the office.

"What was the executive teams' reaction when you responded to the president's justification of the significant losses?"

"Blank stares, silence and then acknowledgment to their egregious oversight," Abe replied.

"What resulted from this very expensive tuition payment?" I asked.

With a huge grin, Abe replied, "Excellent retort. This was a very expensive tuition payment. The good news was it served as a very valuable lesson to the president and the entire executive staff. Together, they delivered many additional years of tremendous profits. Although expensive, the lesson did provide a significant return."

The Future of Our Country

"The future of our country will be built on the backs of independent thinkers. Our economy is dependent on the growth derived from new innovations, skills, expertise, ideas and beliefs. We are about to enter an age where technology will change on a daily basis, all of which, will be led by independent thinkers. They will create the products and services that will change our lives for the better. Greater efficiencies, convenience, social interaction on a global scale, cost savings; these are just some of the positive changes you will see.

I predict that the ratio of successful vs. unsuccessful will continue to widen. There will be a great demarcation of those who will achieve great prosperity and those that will barely survive, living paycheck to paycheck."

"Why such a vast chasm in prosperity?" I asked.

Abe replied, "Because most will be shackled by fear, self-doubt and worry while they try and adapt to the fast-paced environment. Stagnation and mental paralysis will be part of their normal everyday routine. This inactivity will lead to reliance on others and dependency on the masses. Failure and conformity are all but certain. Most will voluntarily surrender the most alienable right they have, freedom of thought and expression, all as a result from the most debilitating emotions known to mankind, fear and worry."

I could tell Abe was extremely passionate about this topic. The mere thought of allowing someone else to make decisions for him was irritating. He couldn't understand why anyone would relinquish this all-encompassing power; freedom of thought.

Abe continued, "Conversely, independent thinkers, are people of courage, unafraid to make decisions and accept the consequences which follow; good or bad. They will lead us into the future. At first, these independent thinkers will be labeled odd or strange. Their ideas will be shunned, but mark my words, this will change quickly! These ideas will transform the globe with products and services which change the way we live at a fundamental level."

Activity vs. Accomplishment

"Before we conclude today's lesson, please understand **that activity is not accomplishment**. Most people fill up their day with all types of inefficient tasks. So for your assignment, I simply want you to carve out twenty minutes a day, once in the morning and once in the evening and do nothing but think. In the evening session I want you to think about all of the actions you took for that day. Did you accomplish what you set out to do? What did you learn? How can you use the day's events to create a better tomorrow?"

"Why do people use activity as accomplishment? I asked.

"Because most people want to do, and not *think*. Doing provides a sense of accomplishment. Thinking conversely is not measurable. You don't see results immediately. But as we've discussed, your thoughts are the genesis of where every great discovery starts. Thoughts lead to ideas and strategies and the transformation of these ideas and strategies into reality. You must take the time to think every day and then act on those thoughts. Dream big and *act!*"

And with that, our session concluded.

Whenever I reflect on this lesson, I'm amazed at Abe's clairvoyance. In the new millennium, think about all the changes occurring in the first two decades.

Greater efficiencies=Transactional reporting at work with tools such as IPADS

Convenience=Online shopping

Social interaction on a global scale-Smart phones and social media

Cost savings=Cloud based solutions reducing the need for expensive hardware

The Assignment

Read and refresh your understanding of the following principles around Independent Thinking:

1) Rely on your **own** thoughts to succeed; utilize your imagination and be as creative as you can. All ideas are born from a strong imagination and lead to 'Playing Big.'

2) Have confidence and believe in yourself and in your decisions.

3) Stay away from the masses.

4) The most 'abnormal', or original ideas, result in life changing products and services.

And then:

1) Carve out twenty minutes a day, once in the morning and once in the evening, **to think**.

2) In the evening session, list all of the actions you planned for the day. Put a check by the ones you accomplished and how they will help you tomorrow. Write out why the others were not accomplished, and what you learned.

3) In the evening, list all of your planned events/tasks you wish to accomplish. Are there any impediments? Jot down some possible solutions.

Symphony No. 13
Conquering 'Time Villains'

"Time is the one element in life where every person is allotted the same amount to accomplish the actions necessary to achieve a defined purpose."

Driving back to Baltimore, I just kept thinking- *what a great lesson!* **Activity is not accomplishment**. As that idea sunk in, I realized I was using the *quantity* of activity to measure the *quality* of my day, which are two entirely different things. It was centered on completing everything on my 'to do' list rather than making sure the important tasks were completed well, setting myself up for the next day.

So I immediately began to carve out twenty minutes a day, once in the morning and once in the evening and do nothing but *think*. I put these twenty minute blocks on my calendar and soon, it was a habit. Almost immediately I noticed:

✓ I was accomplishing so much more in less time.

✓ Any setbacks were now being accounted for and used as a learning experience rather than brushing off and forgotten.

✓ I was using the current day's events to create a more efficient and effective tomorrow.

✓ I was more prepared and therefore less anxious about uncertain outcomes.

✓ I was more focused on my vision and purpose for the day.

✓ I was achieving goals much quicker than I anticipated.

I knew I was laying down a great foundation for incredible long-term success; brick by brick by brick. I was excited to share this with Abe as the next session approached. That Saturday, I felt the wind beneath my wings as I coasted into New York City. After our customary greeting, that was Abe's first question.

"Did you make good time on your trip here?"

"I did. Very little traffic; took me only three hours to get here..."

"I'm glad to hear that, especially because our lesson today is centered on time; the one element in life that is a constant. Every person is allotted the same amount of hours in a day to accomplish the actions necessary to achieve a defined purpose."

"I love how you lead into a lesson," I chuckled, "there is a method to everything you do. It amazes me."

Abe smiled and brushed off my compliment as if his gift of mentoring and teaching was no big deal.

"Before we start today's lesson, are you taking time to *think* twice a day?"

"I am Abe, once in the morning and once in the evening..." I went onto explain in detail the benefits I derived from this exercise and the wonderful habits I was creating. Abe was very pleased and extremely impressed that I took the time to schedule it on my calendar. It showed him a great commitment to one of the most important exercises of the day, taking the time <u>to think</u> before acting.

Father Time

"Young man, as I just mentioned to you, time is a currency we all receive; twenty-four hours in a day- every day. Time doesn't discriminate, it's not dependent on how much money you have and it's available in the same quantity for everyone. Mastering the art of time, and making sure 'Time Villains' don't take it from you, will lead to great productivity and wealth. Ignore it, and it will lead to stagnation and failure.

Mastering time management is not easy. Most of us feel invincible and immortal, believing we will out-live Father Time. Nothing could be farther from the truth. As you get older, time feels like it passes more quickly. Before I knew it, my kids were off to college and my wife and I were empty-nesters. Then, in another blink of an eye, my kids were married living in different states and we were grandparents.

It just goes by so quickly, so it is your obligation to make every second of each day count."

"Abe, managing time seems so basic and logical but most, including myself, have such a difficult time staying disciplined so that we can make every second of the day count. I find that right after hearing about a tragic event where someone I know has passed away, reminds me to rethink time again. That's when it hits home; life is fleeting and we should all make the most of it."

"That's exactly right. It takes something tragic to remind us how short our time is on this earth. You should live each day as if it's your last! So, I'm going to cover a series of strategies that will help you master Father Time..."

Taking the Time to Think

"Let's revisit last month's homework assignment and the importance of taking the time to think. Most people fill up their day with all types of inefficient tasks because the vast majority of people want to do and not think. Thinking provides you with an opportunity to reexamine and reflect back on the actions you took for that day. Did you accomplish what you set out to do? What did you learn? How can you use the day's events to create a better tomorrow? When you address these questions, you provide yourself with a chance to better yourself and be more efficient and effective tomorrow.

Thinking also allows you to remove yourself from the day to day grind where we find ourselves putting out fires and jumping from task to task without any thought of where we are going. We drift through the sea of life rudderless and with no direction. Having no direction is our Segway into our next time management strategy, which is the genesis, as you know, where all success begins."

Having a Clear and Defined Purpose

"In our very first lesson and throughout our time together, we've discussed how having a clear and defined purpose is the genesis of where every success starts. The overwhelming majority drift aimlessly through life without any conception of what they want to achieve. They haven't the slightest clue of what they want or their objective for which to strive.

So if you haven't a direction or focus, you drift off course and spread your thoughts and time in many different directions. An unfocused, unclear mind leads to weakness, indecision, a lack of time awareness and ultimately, failure.

Having a clear and defined purpose is not only the genesis of where every success begins; it's also the genesis of conquering and properly managing your time. When you have a clear and defined purpose you're focused on what you want and then you can create the road map to lead you there. A defined purpose + your roadmap + taking the right action in the present= effective time management."

Everything made perfect sense so I found myself nodding in agreement while taking voracious notes as Abe spoke. I had no questions. I understood the importance of where the seed of success begins and how it directly impacted every second of my day.

"If you were to live each day as if it's your last, focus on your defined purpose and accomplish your action steps with laser like concentration, you would not have time to think about yesterday or tomorrow. You would focus only on today."

Focus on Today

"Focusing on today is imperative to properly mastering time management. First, make sure you read your success statement twice daily to insure you stay focused on your defined purpose. Also, remember our conversation from our third lesson of *'Being Aware of Your Surroundings.'* Do not waste one moment dwelling on yesterday's perceived failures and setbacks. You've addressed these each night, re-examining the current day's events and seeing these failures and setbacks as learning experiences to make the next day better.

This is a real problem for most people. Instead of moving forward and overcoming setbacks, people feel sorry for themselves and wallow in self-pity. Then they quit.

I once asked a highly successful professional ballplayer I met at a fundraiser the key to his success. While a dogged determination and hard work were the foundation for developing his skills, the one trait he felt provided him with the edge over everyone else was the ability to have a short memory. He never dwelled on a bad play or a mistake. He thought about what he did wrong and how he could use the experience to improve moving forward.

It's no different for the best executives or the top salespeople. Failure only fuels them. Not a moment is given to dwelling on past setbacks. They use their time wisely using these past experiences to continually improve until their defined purpose is achieved.

In addition to dwelling on past setbacks, stop thinking about tomorrow and worrying about 'debts that most likely will never come due' or events that you may never see. These are the negative 'what ifs' that most people think about, which create wasted energy and anxiety.

While you should plan for the future, don't lose sight of how important it is to enjoy the moment you're currently experiencing. These experiences are directly responsible for helping you to mold the future you'd like to attain.

We spend so much time on yesterday and tomorrow that today becomes nothing but a blur. Piece together day after day after day of blurs and you have a lifetime of accomplishing very little. This is a key reason so many experience a mid-life crisis when they reach their middle ages; so little to account for after spending the majority of their lives dwelling on past events and worrying about the problems of tomorrow."

"Abe, isn't dwelling on past events and worrying about the problems of tomorrow, as I've learned, attributable to the adverse habits we form such as guilt and fear?"

"Yes. That's a very astute point. Guilt and fear keep you from living each day to the fullest. In fact, along with guilt and fear you can add worry, self-doubt, indecision and procrastination to the list of time assassins. That's why I refer to them as the deadly enemies of time."

Eliminating Self-Sabotaging Habits

"To live each day to the fullest and with purpose, you must eliminate each of these habits. Based on our previous lessons, you should be able to tell me how to eliminate each one."

"Okay, let me take a shot..."

Guilt: To conquer guilt, don't dwell on past mistakes that you can't change. Accept the mistakes and embrace them as opportunities to grow and transform yourself into a better person. Also, don't let guilt affect your ability to make decisions. Make decisions and live with the consequences.

Fear and worry: To conquer fear and worry you must have courage, the willingness to confront your fear and continue to move forward and persevere. When you have courage, you're unafraid to make mistakes because you know that failures are nothing more than temporary defeats.

Self-Doubt: To conquer self-doubt, you must have an unrelenting faith and belief in yourself as well as your defined purposes.

Indecision: To conquer indecision, be an independent thinker, make decisions and live with the consequences, favorable or unfavorable, understanding that even if it's unfavorable, you've just learned something new that will help you in the future. You cannot succeed without temporary setbacks and failures, which can only occur when you make decisions and act.

Procrastination: To conquer procrastination, again it's all about action. You must take the right action in the present. Action is the cure all for procrastination, mental paralysis and stagnation.

"Well done, young man. I should let you teach the rest of the lesson."

"No thanks... I'm much more comfortable being the student."

Mastering the Day

"Abe, how do you deal with all the interruptions during the day, even when you have a good 'game plan'?"

"I assume you're referring to the interruptions occurring throughout the day at work. Is that correct?"

"Exactly."

"You must master the day and not allow the day to master you."

"I'm not sure I understand..."

"Mastering the day means taking control of how your day progresses...let me explain..."

Task List

"I begin mastering my day the night before. That's when I create my list of action steps which need to be completed over the next day, organized in order of priority. I do this for several reasons. First, it allows me to sleep better knowing I'm prepared and organized. Second, as soon as I awaken, I'm ready to take action and not waste one moment of the day. One important point I want to note is that I never take on more than I believe I can handle. Knowing your limitations is extremely important. When you take on too much, you become overwhelmed, stagnate and accomplish nothing.

Next, I begin each day by attacking the most difficult tasks first. For non-essential tasks, complete them after hours or during a set time on the weekends. Completing the non-essential tasks first provide you with a false sense of accomplishment and may awaken the procrastination villains."

Checking Messages and Meetings

"Throughout the day I minimize my distractions by setting aside two to three scheduled times a day to check my voice mail and return phone messages, unless it's an absolute emergency." [Today it's even more important with emails and text messages.]

"How did you handle interruptions within the office such as management and staff members requiring your feedback or opinion?"

"My rule was simple. If it's a true emergency that required my immediate attention, I address it instantly. If it's not, I schedule a time to meet at the earliest time available for both parties. I want to make clear there is a distinct difference between those in my organization and those outside of my organization. For those outside of my organization, I was extremely selective about scheduling a meeting. I'd make sure the meeting added value to myself or my company, especially with someone I've never met with before.

Most people have a tendency to want to please and not offend the other party. However, you must understand your time is precious. It's the most precious asset you have. Once it's gone, it cannot be recovered. So remember, it's okay to politely say *no.* "

"And, may I suggest adding one note to your suggestion Abe?"

"Of course—"

"It's okay to say 'no' and not be adversely affected by the Time Villain, guilt."

"Well said, young man."

"Starting right now, I want you to make every moment count. And your assignment is simple. Apply the series of strategies we've discussed in today's lesson that will help you master father time."

"Abe, I'll start right now. Thanks for another amazing lesson."

The Assignment

Take the time to think and make a plan the night before so that you can focus on the day. This will help you master the day and the Time Villains.

1) Have a clear and defined purpose, the genesis of conquering and properly managing your time.
2) Look at your task list and break it into four parts:
   - ✓ Things you can eliminate
   - ✓ Things you can automate
   - ✓ Things you can delegate
   - ✓ Things that only **you** can concentrate on

Write down the action steps needed in each category so that you can use your time in the most productive way.

Symphony No.14

True Harmony

"Success cannot be achieved without the help of others."

For this month's assignment, the first two strategies were already in motion. I have a clear and defined purpose and was thinking twice a day. The next three needed much attention. I knew it was absolutely imperative to form the habit of reminding myself continually to focus on today; stay in the present and neither dwell on the past nor think about tomorrow. The more I reminded myself, the easier this was to accomplish.

To live each day to the fullest and with purpose, I worked diligently to conquer each of the deadly enemies of time: **guilt, fear and worry, self-doubt, indecision and procrastination**. Additionally, I worked on mastering the day to take control of how my day progressed utilizing the strategies recommended by Abe.

It seems so simple when you read it on paper! But mastering 'Father Time' is one of the most difficult endeavors to maintain over a prolonged period. Our lives are so filled with responsibilities and tasks [particularly in this ever changing and fast- moving world] that we can get lost in a daily grind, side-tracked and not appreciate the moments of our lives.

The Saturday I arrived for our fourteenth session, I knew what his first question would be. I was right.

"How did you fare with your new time management strategies?"

"Well- it's a work in progress..." I sighed.

"And it will continue to be for the rest of your life. However, it will become easier to master the more you focus and are aware of how you spend every moment of each day.

Today we're going to look at Coordinated Cooperative Effort- true harmony, if you will- and how it will help you achieve all that you desire, for you and others. Every highly successful entrepreneur I know has created a culture of orchestrated coordinated cooperative effort. The very foundations of their companies are built on all members working together as a unit to achieve the company's defined purposes. No one person, including the owner[s], is more important than the company. This applies to your life outside of business, as well. Every successful partnership, including your personal relationships, is dependent upon orchestrated coordinated cooperative effort and a harmonious environment."

"How do you *create* this 'true harmony' and this idea that a rising tide lifts all ships in a company?" I asked.

"Engagement and insuring that everyone knows that company goals supersede individual goals," Abe replied. "In order to create this culture of harmony, you need to start with **you.** It's incumbent upon you to show teamwork- enthusiasm, optimism and a confident demeanor. These attributes will then reflect themselves in all who are connected with your company. Remember, *an institution is the lengthened shadow of one man. (Ralph Waldo Emerson).* In other words, it starts with you- the maestro- and your organization will follow your lead."

Orchestrating True Harmony

"Let's revisit for a moment our discussion on the prosperity retreat. During one of our quarterly retreats, we were tasked with solving a problem for one of our participants, Tom, who owned a company that manufactured commercial signs. The company employed several hundred people, was well-known in the industry and was fortunate to have many long-standing customers. On the surface, they should have enjoyed many fruitful years of success. But, that wasn't the case. Due to ongoing production issues, a relatively high employee turnover rate, an unusually large number of employee absences and continuous bickering among the company's employees, the company consistently underachieved.

This was not at all surprising to me. Tom was constantly walking around looking like the weight of the world was on his shoulders, even at our group meetings. He rarely smiled, lacked enthusiasm and energy and rarely engaged his staff as to the company's vision and direction."

"So how did your group help him?"

"The first step was for Tom to recognize that the company's problems began and ended with **him.** He needed to understand that an institution is only as good as the leader at the helm. So- he had two choices… to continue to be apathetic, pessimistic and unengaged with his employees <u>or</u> to change his demeanor to one of enthusiasm, optimism and confidence. Tom needed to change himself to create a positive, harmonious culture throughout the entire organization. Every person must buy into this culture.

Step two was for Tom to engage his staff members by sharing the company's defined purpose and vision. What did the company want to achieve? What are the common goals that everyone must strive in order to be successful? This exercise creates a feeling of ownership with the staff. When management and employees are not in sync, a lack of harmony exists, which will ultimately lead to an ineffective and inefficient organization.

Step three was to make sure all staff members knew the definition of a great and highly valuable employee. The definition of a great and highly valuable employee is one who not only achieves their own personal goals but also helps others throughout the organization achieve theirs as well. Company goals must always supersede personal goals because without the company, no one exists, including the owner.

Step four was for Tom to control his environment and only surround the company with people who are engaged with this process. It only takes one person who is disruptive to weaken the harmony of the organization as a whole.

Finally, step five [and I know you'll recognize this step], shower praise and gratitude on your staff members. Be *grateful* to members of your organization! Each person is important to the success of your company. A happy employee is usually a very productive employee.

Remember these recommendations?"

a) Always listen to their ideas and be grateful and appreciative whether you implement them or not.

b) Show gratitude when they successfully complete a task and share their accomplishments with the rest of the organization.

c) Acknowledge their value and contributions to the organization.

d) Plan company gatherings to celebrate joyous occasions.

e) Treat them to lunch from time to time.

f) Listen attentively and show a genuine and sincere interest when they share information about their personal lives such as their children's achievements.

g) Look for opportunities to enrich their lives. Remember, no act is too small.

h) When mistakes occur, be calm and composed and try to use as an opportunity to teach them something new."

"So let me summarize the steps, Abe..."

Step 1: Change Yourself. Be accountable.

Step 2: Engage your staff members, your team.

Step 3: Insure your team knows the definition of a great employee and how to attain this status.

Step 4: Control your environment. You must create a harmonious culture from top to bottom.

Step 5: Implement the 'Power of Gratitude' with your entire team.

"On the button," Abe replied.

"Did Tom get it right?"

"He did. It took time, but once the culture changed and Tom surrounded himself with people who bought into the new company philosophy, the company's results were dramatically improved. They began to attain a level of success they hadn't seen for many years. Eventually, Tom sold the company for a significant price and retired."

Attaining True and Enduring Power

"When you think of power, what is the first thing you think of?"

I thought for a minute and responded, "Money, fame, status."

"And that's what most people believe," replied Abe. "Money, material objects and fame are just a by-product of true power. True power is when you have a defined purpose backed by the right action and orchestrated coordinated cooperative effort. The formula:

A Defined Purpose + the Right Action + Orchestrated Coordinated Cooperative Effort =True Power

"I see- so when this happens, it will naturally lead to those things we associate with power; money, material objects, status, etc..."

"Yes. Now, if you want to have enduring power- power that lasts in perpetuity- you must add one very key ingredient. That key ingredient is using the power to help and enrich the lives of others. Without this key ingredient, the power attained becomes short-lived."

"Why is it short-lived?"

"Because when you use this power only for your benefit it fails to access the law of unlimited and infinite returns, which only occurs by enriching the lives and helping others. I've seen numerous occurrences where one person has attained enormous wealth only to relinquish it as a result of being self-absorbed, selfish, ostentatious, pretentious and/or conceited. Unfortunately, for many, the loss of wealth is worse than never attaining it, leading to embarrassment and depression."

While he was talking I was thinking, *how fascinating!* All of these principles I was learning now were coming together and cohesively connecting with each other!

The Foundation of Orchestrated
Coordinated Cooperative Effort

"The very essence of orchestrated effort is built on the foundation of integrity, honor, truthfulness and fairness. Everyone must display these characteristics in order to enjoy the fruits of success. Look back at all the successful achievements in history and you will find each is based on orchestrated coordinated cooperative effort. And it's not limited to just business. Sport teams, charitable foundations, new historical discoveries, medical breakthroughs and victories in war all used orchestrated effort."

As a huge sports fan, I now understood how teams became successful and won championships. One of the best examples was the UCLA Bruins basketball team of the 1960's and 1970's under Hall of Fame coach, John Wooden. He won an astounding ten Division I NCAA championships in a twelve year period; including a stretch of seven in a row. No one since then has come close to attaining this level of dominance. When you study Coach Wooden's well-known quotes, there is overwhelmingly one key principle: TEAM.

Quotes from Coach John Wooden:

"The main ingredient of stardom is the rest of the team."

"The best way to improve the team is to improve us."

"The team with the most talent usually wins."

"Team spirit means you are willing to sacrifice personal considerations for the welfare of all. That defines a team player."

"Teamwork is not a preference, it is a requirement."

"Make sure team members know they are working with you, not for you."

"Loyalty is a cohesive force that forges individuals into a team."

"Much can be accomplished by teamwork when no one is concerned about what gets credit."

Personal Relationships

"Most of our conversation today has been focused on true harmony in business, however, as I mentioned at the beginning of our lesson, every successful partnership, including your personal relationships, is dependent upon orchestrated coordinated cooperative effort and a harmonious environment. The most successful relationships, including your marriage, are centered on strong communication and working cohesively together in tandem with integrity, honor, truthfulness and fairness.

There is no stronger feeling of encouragement than to know your spouse supports you and your defined purposes.

That is why it is so important to engage and have an ongoing dialogue to support each other's endeavors. Too often, I hear stories of a lack of communication where one feels alone, like they are on a desert island with no one in sight. When I ask about their spouse and why they feel alone, their response is usually, '*My spouse doesn't understand what I'm going through [or the issues/problems] that I incur on a daily basis.*' My response to that is; 'have you taken the time to engage and explain the issues to your spouse? Have you really made the effort to include them and share with them your defined purposes and action steps? Have you asked for their input on why you're experiencing failure or setbacks on a particular initiative? Have you given them the opportunity to help you?' Their retort is usually, '*No. I don't have the time or energy to explain what I'm experiencing. She/he wouldn't understand anyway.*' Take the time to explain. Let them be a part of and engage them in the process. You'll be surprised how well they understand, albeit from a totally different perspective; one you may not have given thought to."

I know from firsthand experience how important a spouse can be. I attribute much of my success to my wife, Bobbie. She may not have the business experience I possess but her knack for common sense solutions to problems has led to many a successful outcome. It took me a few years to realize the importance of this orchestrated effort, but now having her by my side is my greatest weapon.

"Now for your assignment, I want you to start utilizing the five steps, as Tom did, modifying them to fit the different areas of your life; business, personal, etc. Start laying the groundwork now for true and enduring power," Abe added with a smile. And with that, our incredible session on true harmony and coordinated cooperative effort was complete.

The Assignment

Under each of these steps, write down three things you can do to accomplish them.

✓ Step 1: Change Yourself. Be accountable.

✓ Step 2: Engage your staff members, your team.

✓ Step 3: Insure your team knows the definition of a great employee and how to attain this status.

✓ Step 4: Control your environment. You must create a harmonious culture from top to bottom.

✓ Step 5: Implement the 'Power of Gratitude' with your entire team.

Symphony No.15

The Passion Piece

"Passion is a critical force that energizes a person to accomplish at least twice as much work as one can usually perform without becoming fatigued."

When I returned to Baltimore, I immediately started working on the 5 steps in the assignment. Because this assignment incorporated several previous lessons, I felt the foundation was laid for a smooth transition to create a culture of orchestrated coordinated cooperative effort, and therefore going into session 16, I felt pretty good. Of course, Abe wanted to know where I was in the process.

"So," he asked, "is your company coming together as one?"

"It is. Engaging the employees is genius! They feel a sense of ownership when their ideas are heard and they inherently get more involved as we all work towards a common goal. I must admit, I felt like I had a head start based on the previous lessons of accountability, controlling my environment and orchestrated coordinated cooperative effort."

"I knew you would. It's one of the most important pillars in order to build a successful organization. Now, I have a very important question for you. Do you *love* what you do?"

"Of course... Why do you ask?"

"Because, whenever you engage in a defined purpose, success occurs much more frequently and swiftly when the purpose is backed by underline passion. Passion is a powerful emotion and is the **E-Motion=energy in motion-** and critical in propelling a person forward so that they may accomplish twice as much as someone who is not enthusiastic about their defined purpose. Few business owners [and people in general] consistently enjoy their work. This ultimately leads to an unsatisfied, empty feeling tied to a lack of accomplishment because their passion is unsustainable. So- I have to ask that question to make sure you are passionate about the goals and achievements you are pursuing today. Otherwise, you're going to have a difficult time going the distance on the current path you've chosen."

"Abe, I can assure you, I am passionate about my defined purposes and I look forward each day to taking the right actions in the present, putting me one step closer to achievement."

"That's great to hear because passion and an unrelenting faith to succeed is a very powerful formula to achieving great success."

Passion + Unrelenting Faith to Succeed = A Very Powerful Formula to Achieving Great Success

Changing Your Roadmap

"Abe, can you remember a time when you weren't passionate about a current undertaking? And if so, what did you do?"

"Yes, many times. For example, when I commit to being a board member for a philanthropic organization, I like to become engaged and involved in helping the organization succeed and prosper. However, there have been occasions where I did not agree with the direction of that board and therefore I lost my passion. When I'm not passionate about something, I simple move on so I don't waste my time.

This has also occurred in 'for profit' companies as well. About twenty years ago, we purchased a retail company which sold equipment and accessories for the outdoorsman. This was not a typical purchase for us as our portfolios specialized in non-retail companies. However, because of my love for the outdoors, particularly fishing, I made an exception. Within four months of the purchase, I realized we made a mistake. We didn't have the right people in place to oversee the company and I lacked the passion to commit the necessary time it required to be successful."

"What did you do?"

"I sold it, incurred a small loss and moved on to other initiatives."

"Were you upset that you lost money on this transaction?"

"Not at all. It was the *tuition I had to pay* in order to learn this lesson; do not let initial personal excitement cloud your judgement when it comes to making a business decision. If I had taken the time to study the financial statements and the potential earnings of the company rather than listen to my bias towards the outdoors, I never would have purchased the company in the first place. However, once I realized I didn't have the passion to continue, I quickly took action, sold the business and moved on to other endeavors.

Time Management's Best Friend

"There is a very important lesson in this last sentence, one I want you to remember in perpetuity. Passion is time management's best friend."

"I'm not sure I understand, Abe…"

"To better understand, let me quote from arguably our greatest president, Abraham Lincoln, who said:

'Every man is proud of what he does well; and no man is proud of what he does not do well. With the former, his heart is in his work; and he will do twice as much of it with less fatigue. The latter performs a little imperfectly, looks at it in disgust, turns from it, and imagines himself exceedingly tired. The little he has done, comes to nothing, for want of finishing.'

When your heart is in your work, when you possess **passion,** you accomplish twice as much with less fatigue. You become the master of your day instead of the day mastering you. You enjoy the journey more because you can't wait to get started each and every day. You can teach time management strategies all day long to a business owner, however, if they lack passion for their work or service, these strategies ultimately prove ineffective."

The Enemy of Fear

"In addition to being time management's best friend, passion is one of the conquerors of fear. Passion drives you to succeed because you're so enthused with what you're doing, you don't have time to think about failure. When you are totally immersed in taking the right action, the energy you're expending becomes effortless and exponential. Passionate action is transparent and will influence everyone around you."

The Passion-less Business Owner

"Abe, let's go back a minute to your example of the company you purchased in the retail business of selling equipment and accessories for the outdoorsman. You realized you lacked passion for continuing the venture and got out without any major obstacles or barriers. However, I'm sure there are many business owners who lack passion for their business, but they can't just stop because it's the only source of income supporting their family. What do you tell <u>them</u>?"

"That's a great question and you're exactly correct. Just as passionate action is transparent, so is the lack of it. Most people can't hide behind it before you see disgust, frustration and fatigue emerge in people. They feel 'stuck' operating a company without any enthusiasm. Speak to that person and you will often hear the phrases, *'I'm so tired,' 'I just want to get out,' 'No one understands the troubles I have...'* or *'It's always one thing after the next...'*

When this occurs, instead of wallowing in self-pity, take the following action steps:

a. Define what it is you are passionate about. This is your defined purpose.

b. Determine whether you can incorporate this purpose into your current business.

c. If this is not possible, begin planning and taking the necessary action steps for converting this purpose into reality while you continue in your current line of work.

d. If necessary, pursue these plans late at night [after work] so you can continue to make money in your current line of work to support your family. If you are truly passionate, the long hours will not deter you.

e. Procrastination is the deadly enemy of progress, but if you have incredible passion, nothing will stand in your way of making plans for a new passion-filled life.

A Necessary Component of Orchestrated Effort

"Abe, in the previous lesson you told me in order to achieve orchestrated effort in your company, you must show enthusiasm and optimism at all times. So based on this lesson, passion is a necessary component of orchestrated effort?"

"Absolutely, great point! You must instill passion in your team members in order for your organization to thrive. Let me outline how I created passion for our team members…"

a) Create the right culture. Again, it all starts with you and your attitude. You must be perceived as an excited, enthusiastic leader. Even on your most stressful days, your outward appearance must be one of optimism and cheerfulness.

b) Get to know all your team members and what excites them. This provides you with valuable information so you can incorporate responsibilities and tasks, which motivates them to succeed.

c) Provide opportunities for your team members to advance and show them how to achieve.

d) Surround yourself with the right people who instill the same passion as you, especially your entire management team.

e) Place more emphasis on hiring people who are driven and committed to excel. The passion they exude will clearly come through in your interview.

f) Apply the lesson on the 'Power of Gratitude' to members of your organization as we discussed.

"Since you already have tremendous passion for your company, for this month's assignment, I'd like you to implement these steps to insure your entire team is passionate and engaged in helping you to achieve your defined purposes. Again, lay the groundwork for a world-class impassioned organization."

"I'm impassioned to start," I smiled slyly. He smiled back.

"See you next month, young man."

The Assignment

1) Create an engaging culture: Show up with a great attitude, be an excited, enthusiastic leader.

2) Get to know all your team members and what excites them.

3) Provide opportunities for your team members to advance and show them how to achieve.

4) Surround yourself with the productive, supportive people who have the same passion and drive to reach peak potential.

5) Place more emphasis on hiring people who are driven and passionate about their work and purpose.

6) Infuse the 'Power of Gratitude' into all aspects of your business; especially the members of your organization.

Symphony No.16
Prelude to Tomorrow

"Every problem can be turned into an opportunity if you're properly prepared."

Starting with myself, I immediately began to implement the steps necessary to insure our culture was one of excitement, enthusiasm and engagement. My mission was to make sure- even on the most stressful days- I greeted our staff members with a smile. My outward appearance never vacillated from optimism and cheerfulness. Given the fact that I was one of those people who 'wear their emotions on their sleeve,' this was not an easy transition.

Next, I engaged each staff member in conversation to find out what excites them and motivates them to succeed. Once the information was gathered, I began to work with the management team to create individual plans providing opportunity for advancement. Each plan consisted of action steps for them to accomplish in order to achieve specific goals and expectations. We then met with each person to review their plan. Most importantly, every day I applied the 'Power of Gratitude' and made sure our management team did so as well.

[It should be noted that although there wasn't a need to hire anyone new that particular month; I continue to only hire people who are driven, committed and have a burning passion to excel in their field of expertise.]

At our sixteenth session I arrived full of excitement! I wanted to tell Abe how quickly our culture was changing and the changes I was seeing in *myself.*

"Good morning, Abe."

"Good morning, young man. Are you prepared to discuss your assignment on orchestrated coordinated cooperative effort?" Abe said with a sheepish grin.

Abe had that look that said 'I'm asking a leading question to prepare you for today's lesson.'

"I know that look," I said.

"We'll see if you're right... proceed with your assignment," Abe said with a smile.

For the next fifteen minutes, I spoke about the immediate action steps I took to improve the culture; shifting it to one of excitement, enthusiasm and optimism. I could see Abe was impressed and especially proud of the work I was doing on me.

"As usual, a job well done." replied Abe. "You certainly were prepared for today's lesson...outstanding work!"

I noticed again he kept emphasizing the word 'prepared.' *What was that all about?*

"Now, for today's lesson; prepare for the events of tomorrow, today."

"I see; it's all making sense..." I added.

"In order to attain success in business and in life, you must be properly prepared for the events of tomorrow <u>today</u>. This means, you are prepared for anything that may, or may not, occur in the future.

Being unprepared is analogous to 'working in the dark' or 'operating blindly.' When you operate a company blindly you risk being caught off guard, which can cause major disruptions, or in some cases, the inability to continue in business. In life, it works the same way. If you don't prepare, you're at great risk to suffer unfavorable consequences."

Surprises are not Excuses for Failures

"One should never have surprises in business and in most cases, life. Surprises are not excuses for failure. When you're prepared for the events of tomorrow today, you have a set of action plans ready to combat the 'so-called' surprises. Do you recall when we discussed the fear of uncertainty, or the unknown, in the lesson on courage?"

"Of course...it's the one fear I obsessed about the most, which has caused the majority of my anxiety."

"And, I mentioned that in today's world, there is a great deal of uncertainty facing everyone, which is bound to cause most to either retreat or remain stagnant." Abe added. "Do you also remember the steps I recommended to manage this uncomfortable feeling of anxiety?"

"Yes. You have to attack the uncertainty head on, learning as much about the issues causing your concern. Once you understand the issues underneath your concerns, you're ready to plan appropriately and prepare accordingly." *As I absorbed the last line, I started to slow down my thoughts realizing that this was the foundation of today's lesson.*

"Exactly- Those that prepare properly experience much less anxiety because the uncertainties are no longer so frightening."

Being properly prepared=One of the greatest ways to help reduce anxiety.

"Abe, I completely understand the theory of preparing for the events of tomorrow *today*, however, from a practical standpoint, how do you implement this philosophy? In other words, how do you identify all of the different scenarios to prepare for?"

"That's a great question. Revisit what I said when we started this lesson: Being unprepared is analogous to working in the dark or operating blindly. When you operate a company blindly you risk being "caught off guard,' which can cause major disruptions or in some cases, the inability to continue in business. So you must consistently ask yourself two questions:

a) What can cause major disruptions?
b) What can cause a discontinuation of the business?

"I actually created a checklist of possible scenarios which I use as a reminder, so I am prepared. I have a copy which I'll provide you in just a minute. Before we continue, there is a basic, yet overlooked rule that every entrepreneur must follow. You'll know this one well; *know your numbers!*"

Know Your Numbers

"You could probably teach this part of the lesson," Abe said with a smile.

"Yes- this is right in my comfort zone. Quite frankly, I never understood how any entrepreneur could <u>not</u> know their numbers and expect to succeed. It's the greatest example of, as you said, 'operating blindly.' How can you have a clear vision, a defined purpose, without knowing where you currently are and where you want to go? Knowing your numbers is the ultimate roadmap. If you don't mind, I'd like to share the advice I gave every business owner when I was a Certified Public Accountant."

"No, by all means, go right ahead..."

The Four Step Process to Know Your Numbers

"First, you need to make sure the books and records are up to date. This means an up-to-date Profit and Loss Statement and a Balance Sheet. I define 'up-to-date' as having accurate numbers for the current month by the 10th day of the subsequent month. This means you have ten days to close out the month so the information is still current and fresh and decisions can be made in real time.

Second, you must review, analyze and understand what the numbers are saying. The numbers tell a story. They don't lie. Good or bad, once you understand the story, you can formulate immediate proactive decisions."

I could see Abe was enjoying listening to me as he sat back in his Victorian chair, hands locked behind his head. He knew all of it, but hearing it from me - a topic I knew really well - was pleasing him. Also, just watching him as he sat and listened provided me with another very valuable lesson. Even though he knew the importance of knowing your numbers and the value of current data, he just listened and nodded his head in approval, never interrupting once. Subsequent to our lesson, I asked him if his silence was a test to see if I really knew what I was talking about. His response was that his 'active listening' was out of courtesy and he hoped to learn something new, which he did. *Imagine that?* Even with all of his success, the teacher was hoping to learn from his student.

"Third, compare your actual monthly results to your projected/budgeted results and analyze any material fluctuations. When I refer to 'projected results,' I'm talking about a projected annual profit and loss and cash flow statement that 'paint the picture' of where you envision the company for the subsequent year. Abe, I can tell you from first-hand experience that very few business owners take the time to prepare for the following year with projected statements and it's a big mistake."

"Why do you think most business owners you speak to don't take the time to utilize this vital tool?" Abe asked.

"Two reasons. They look at it as an exercise in futility because they're just projections and not real numbers, not realizing that those numbers can actually be achieved with the five steps learned in the very first lesson. And, they don't know how because no one is showing them how to create one."

"But being in the accounting field, don't most accountants recommend and help to create them for their clients?" Abe asked.

"Some do and some don't. It depends on who you ask. One accountant I spoke to thinks projections are "only worth the paper they're written on," so it's safe to say they're not recommending it for their clients."

"Well, you're right on target with understanding how important they are."

"Thanks," I said as I continued. "The fourth step is to compare your actual monthly results to your projected results and analyze any material fluctuations."

Use these questions to clarify:

a) Are sales consistent with what you expected?
b) Are costs being controlled properly?
c) Is your profit where you need it to be in order to attain your annual goal?
d) Are your advertising strategies providing a proper return on investment?

"Performing this four step process every month consistently will immensely help any business owner operate their company properly. And, one other point I want to make before I turn the reins over to you again Abe, and that is this exercise is also very important for people <u>who aren't business owners.</u> Creating a personal budget of income and expenses and reviewing every month helps one to be aware of their spending habits and save money for future plans."

"Well done, young man. I enjoyed the break. Now let me pick up from there and revisit how to prepare for these two questions:

a)   What can cause major disruptions?
b)   What can lead to a discontinuation of the business?

"Business continuity is making sure that the company can continue after a major disaster or crisis. The goal is to have the necessary procedures in place so your company is able to continue during and after a disaster. As I mentioned, I created a checklist that I use to constantly remind me what I need to prepare for. Here is your copy..."

Abe handed me a copy. At the top it read: ***Business Continuity.*** The checklist was a compilation of potential disruptions and a brief explanation of each. Some examples are listed below:

a)   Natural disasters- fires, earthquakes, tornados, floods or flash floods, hurricanes, hail storms and winter storms

b) Environmental and regulatory affairs-compliance with agencies such as the OSHA
c) Losing a major customer
d) Losing a major supplier
e) Possible loss of key personnel; including yourself
f) Litigation
g) Economic Events: depression, recession, inflation
h) Internal Events: a chemical spill, an explosion, a power outage
i) Intentional crime/theft
j) Technology Event: a computer crash due to viruses, electrical surges, data corruption or loss of hardware and software due to natural disaster/ fire

"Recall from our lesson on independent thinking and the large heating and air conditioning company with multiple locations across the Mid-Atlantic region..." Abe continued, "...the company's management team didn't prepare for the harsh winter weather and paid the price. If they prepared for the events of tomorrow *today*, they would have recognized the opportunity to form key alliances with companies who thrive during winter storms and called customers not covered by their preventive maintenance plans, a highly profitable recurring revenue source."

Several years later, I would learn this lesson the hard way. Most of our products were shipped to our customers through UPS (United Parcel Service). UPS is a major supplier and they went on strike, which created a huge problem because other carriers would not accept new customers due to the overload of new business they were now receiving. This created a large backorder of products and adversely affected our bottom line. Fortunately, the strike was short-lived and operations normalized quickly. Subsequent to the strike, I immediately called FedEx and utilized them for half of our shipping business. Each carrier would now serve as a backup to prevent this from reoccurring.

As we concluded this month's lesson, Abe tasked me with my new assignment and I was on my way back to Baltimore.

The Assignment

1) Review the Business Continuity Checklist
2) Make a list of any events that could lead to major disruptions and/or a discontinuation of the business and an action plan to counter each one.
3) Create a Profit and Loss and Cash Flow Projection based on where you envision your business in the future.

[Download my simplified templates for Profit and Loss as well as Cash Flow from my web site and begin to fill them out: www.markluterman.com.]

Symphony No. 17

Believe in Your Song

"People will only believe in you when you believe in yourself."

I spent the three-hour ride back home thinking about every event that could possibly lead to a major disruption and/or a discontinuation of my business. Upon arriving home, with the assistance of Abe's Business Continuity Checklist, I compiled a list of events I believed could adversely affect our company. The list was quite significant and overwhelming; eliciting feelings of anxiousness and worry about how susceptible we are to an abrupt life-changing incident.

However, once I began to plan for each event, the anxiety began to dissipate. Once again, Abe was right! When you prepare properly, you experience much less anxiety because the uncertainties are now manageable and, therefore, less frightening. I arrived for our seventeenth session ready and prepared to review my list and the plan associated with each.

"Good morning, young man. You're looking quite confident this morning. I'm assuming you've spent some time thinking about a business continuity plan?"

"I have. I spent the month compiling a list of events which could adversely affect my company and the staff and a continuity plan associated with each one. I hope I didn't miss anything...let me tell you about just a few..."

For the next thirty plus minutes, I explained each contingency plan. Abe offered several recommendations, but overall he seemed quite pleased with the continuity plan. There were two examples in particular that impressed him.

The first was my action plan to acquire spare machinery parts [in case of failure] because the lead time to re-order and receive these components was greater than two days. If one of these parts broke, the entire assembly line would come to a screeching halt! This would be a small disaster, so my plan was to spend approximately $10,000 to inventory these components and avoid having to shut down our production line.

The second was a detailed list of backup suppliers for every raw material used by the company. If a raw material were to be discontinued, production of one or more of our products would cease. A back-up supplier for each material was critical.

"When you first walked in, I mentioned how you were looking quite confident this morning. Today's lesson is all about confidence and believing in yourself." Darn! The lead-up to today's lesson! I totally missed it!

Abe continued, "In order to be successful you must be self-assured, look the part and believe in YOU. I define self - assurance as being 100% secure and confident in your abilities to succeed. It should never be publicized to others as your actions will provide all the proof needed. Let others speak about your accolades and expertise. Be aware of how you talk about yourself; you may be perceived as egotistical as opposed to self-assured. However, a good first impression is critical to success and prosperity. We form opinions, right or wrong, in the first few seconds of meeting someone. How you present yourself is a direct reflection on you and your company.

Self-assurance is born from the ability to have complete and unwavering confidence in your ability to succeed which stem from real accomplishments and a track record that cannot be denied. Genuine confidence, not an act, resides in people who have created resilience and who know that whatever happens, they will rise to the top. Lack of true confidence, or a poor attempt, is easily recognized by others.

People will only believe in your song when they believe you are its sole composer. This is particularly important when you are the leader of a company or organization. If you want them to follow your direction, you must always be accountable and self-assured in your vision, your goals [and the action steps to follow] which will lead to victory.

Accountability + Self Assurance = Effective Leadership

"Abe, what is the best way to gain that real confidence so you can be self-assured?"

"Go back to the very first lesson, 'The First Notes' and the five steps. Once you've defined your purpose, you must have faith and belief that you will achieve it. Remember, self-doubt can never be present. If you have faith that you will achieve your defined purpose backed by the right action steps, which you've developed with a well thought out organized action plan, you've laid the foundation for having unwavering confidence. If you believe in your plans— and you— others will follow.

Also remember as part of the first lesson the principle of self-suggestion. It's the communication link between the conscious and subconscious minds. The dominate thoughts of the conscious mind reach the subconscious mind and influence it with suggestions, whether they are **positive or negative**. So you must continue to fill your mind with confident thoughts and the belief that **you will succeed** no matter what. Again, self-doubt is the antithesis to confidence.

Additionally, our last lesson plays a large role is promoting self-assurance. When you're properly prepared with a real action plan, you are much more confident in your ability to succeed. Does that make sense?"

"It does. I can imagine addressing the company and being self-assured, but what about other scenarios such as walking into a networking event and meeting people? Can you tell when you meet someone whether they're self-assured or lack confidence?"

"Absolutely, within seconds. Aside from how they dress, which we'll discuss shortly, here are some tell- tale signs of people who are self-assured and confident."

a) They walk upright, shoulders back, head upright, as opposed to hunched over and head down

b) They look you square in the eyes; eyes never wandering

c) They greet you with a secure, but not overly firm or soft handshake

d) They speak little of themselves and their accomplishments

e) They listen intently and ask questions, showing an interest in what you have to say

f) Silence in between dialogue does not bother them

g) They speak in an even and moderate pace

h) They smile often and look relaxed

I made sure to highlight this list and regularly review it to remind myself of the importance of people's perception.

Decision - Making

"People who are self-assured are also highly effective decision makers. Remember, everyone has an absolute responsibility and the power within them to make decisions. Those who make good decisions are eventually rewarded with accomplishing whatever it is they desire. When you possess self-assurance, your decisions are based on your own thoughts, opinions and judgements. You don't rely on 'gospel' and propaganda… or care about what others think or do. A lack of self-confidence coincides with procrastination, one of the Time Villains. People who are fearful, and have self-doubt, procrastinate, stagnate and avoid making decisions. What they don't realize is that the more you make decisions- especially good decisions- the more your confidence will grow.

Please understand, self-assurance <u>does not</u> mean you have to have all the answers immediately. If you're not sure of something, it's okay to get back to the person asking the question. Your admission of not being 100% certain is a great example of being confident and secure in your abilities."

An Appearance that Leads

"When I mention the word 'appearance,' what's the first thing that comes to your mind?" Abe asked.

"Your physical appearance; how you look, how you're dressed…etc.," I replied.

"How you dress, how you're groomed- looking the part is an extremely important component of self-assurance. But before we talk about physical appearance, it's important to understand the role your thoughts play in how you look and how you're perceived. We've talked about the importance of thought, the power of self-suggestion and how positive thoughts lead to positive outcomes and negative thoughts lead to negative outcomes. What we haven't spoken about is how your thoughts affect how you *look*.

Thoughts affect the posture of your body, how you walk, how you speak, how persuasive you are as well as your facial expressions. Thoughts also affect the type of people you attract. Like minds attract one another. If you want to attract positive people, if you want others to follow your lead, if you want to be perceived as the expert and leader in your chosen field of practice, you must maintain a positive attitude at all times. Negativity deters people from wanting to be around you."

"Abe, I never really considered how my thoughts were being perceived by others. I tend to 'wear my emotions on my sleeve' so I can only imagine all the times I have discouraged others from associating with me," I said with a sigh.

"That's why it's crucial you understand this lesson if you want to cultivate consistent, ongoing success in the future. Two words which no one should ever ask you are, ' _What's wrong?_' These two words- _what's wrong_- indicate that your facial expressions, body posture and energy all show concern, worry and distress."

"Abe, I've heard those two words quite often and don't like it when people ask me…but I realize now they won't ask if I don't give them a reason to ask."

"That's right. If you don't want to hear it, change your thoughts and your outward appearance will change as well."

"Abe, speaking of outward appearance, what kind of clothing do you recommend people wear?"

"I recommend always dressing appropriately…"

"What do you mean by _dressing appropriately?_"

"Dressing for the occasion. In other words, if you're attending an event requiring formal attire, wear a neatly pressed suit and tie, or even a tuxedo. If you're attending an informal event, a pair of neatly pressed slacks and button down shirt should suffice."

"What if you're not sure?"

"Take an extra set of clothing with you and keep it in your car; especially a coat and tie. But whatever you wear, make sure you always look neat and well groomed; clothes ironed, never wrinkled, clean shaven, nails filed and clean, and always have great hygiene.

Your physical appearance not only affects how others perceive you, it also impacts how you perceive yourself. Psychologically you feel good when you *look good*. This also pertains to your possessions such as your car and house. Always keep them clean and organized. It has a profound psychological impact on how you feel."

"Abe, I want to revisit your statement about how positive attitude is necessary to being perceived as the expert and leader in your chosen field of practice...please explain."

Self–Assurance, Appearance and Playing Big

"Remember our lesson on Playing Big?" Abe asked.

"I do..."

"You had an incredible idea to leave a lasting legacy for generations to remember. You said that you would like to share the lessons I'm teaching you which I have acquired through my life's work, my successes, and the wisdom I've developed, with people all around the world. You want everyone who is open to using this wisdom to be able to have access to it."

"Absolutely!" I replied.

"Well this requires you to be a leader in the field of self-help and motivational speaking and in order to share this information with people you will need to…"

a) Speak publicly
b) Hold seminars and educational retreats
c) Meet with clients
d) Make appearances in the media
e) Organize prosperity group sessions

"In every one of these action steps, people will only listen, absorb and accept this information if they believe in you. You will need to show up with complete authenticity and, therefore, certainty. People's need for certainty is paramount, so if you can convey THAT, you'll be in good shape. Keep positive and don't bring any self-doubt, and they'll be riveted!"

"I get it, and that's good advice."

"You have your assignment; see you next month where we'll discuss one of my favorite topics."

"Okay! Thanks, Abe."

The Assignment

1) Review the list of tell-tale signs of people who are self-assured and confident every day for the next month. Practice them in every opportunity provided you.

2) Be aware of how you sound when you talk about yourself. Let others speak of your accolades and expertise.

3) Pay very close attention to your appearance every day, always look neat and well groomed; clothes ironed, never wrinkled, clean shaven, nails filed and clean, and impeccable hygiene. Remember that your physical appearance affects how others perceive you <u>and</u> how you perceive *yourself.* [This also pertains to your possessions such as your car and house. Always keep them clean and organized.]

Symphony No.18

Staying on Key

*"We cannot control the actions that others take against us,
however we can control how we react with the one defense that
will never fail you; self-control."*

Every day, subsequent to our last session until our next lesson, I reviewed the list of tell-tale signs of people who are self-assured and confident. From inside the office, to networking events or social outings, I practiced them often. There was one in particular I had to really practice; listening intently and asking questions. On several occasions the person I was speaking with was either engaged in talking about themselves or just flat out boring. However, I saw this as a beneficial learning experience to better myself on two levels:

a) Help me develop much stronger listening skills and demonstrate interest in what others are saying while expressing gratitude.

b) Practicing the art of patience and allowing others to speak of my accomplishments and/or share my accolades.

My favorite part of the assignment was showing up looking neat, well-groomed and organized everywhere I went. Psychologically, I just felt better about myself. I also made sure my office, house and car were kept clean and organized. I arrived for our eighteenth session prepared to review my assignment on self-assurance and appearance. After our customary warm greetings, Abe asked me something which perked my ears up.

"I hope this past month was pleasant for you, devoid of any acrimony?"

"I had a great month," I smiled, "and really enjoyed implementing my assignment." [Okay, so he's never mentioned *acrimony* before...must be a prelude to our lesson. I'm thinking something along the lines of avoiding hostility? Remaining calm?]

For the next fifteen to twenty minutes, I imparted all of my 'ah-ha' moments around the assignment. Abe was particularly impressed with the way I handled folks who talked too much about themselves and how I utilized it as a beneficial learning experience. He chuckled about engaging in conversation with boring, or as he said, 'less than interesting people.' I also made him laugh when I told him my car seemed to drive better after a cleaning.

Staying on Key

"So- ready for today's lesson?" Abe asked.

"I'm very curious!"

"Why so curious? Is it because I mentioned at the end of our last session that it was a favorite topic of mine?"

"That ...and I've noticed when you greet me at the beginning of each session, you ask a question which relates to the upcoming lesson; sort of like a clue."

"And what was today's clue?" Abe asked with a grin.

"If this past month was pleasant for me, devoid of any acrimony..."

"And how do you think that question relates to today's lesson?"

"You've never asked me that question before... so I'm thinking today's lesson is along the lines of avoiding hostility? Remaining calm? Am I close?"

"Nicely done! Today's lesson is self-control."

"So please tell me; why is this a favorite topic of yours?"

"Because, as I mentioned to you previously, when I was younger, I possessed a short and unpredictable temper. It took many years, some very difficult lessons and a real commitment to maintaining self-control. I'm very proud of this accomplishment, as it has contributed significantly to my personal and business successes. In fact, one of my favorite quotes is from the great philosopher Plato:

The first and best victory is to conquer Self.

"Conquering yourself, or 'staying on key,' can only be achieved once you attain complete self-control. You must master the emotion of anger and hatred and never retaliate, ever! Self-control is an extremely powerful weapon-and the great part is-everyone possesses it. Unfortunately, few choose to use it. It's available at any time, and when used properly, can generate an inordinate amount of value and benefit. All successful people, without exception, exhibit self-control in every situation they encounter."

"If it's available for everyone to use, why do so few people, me included, choose to ignore it?" I was sincerely wondering how to use this to my advantage.

"Because, most people do not take control of their thoughts, and subsequently, their actions. Think about a time when someone said, or did something, you didn't like. What's the first thought that comes to your mind?"

"They're disrespecting me... or taking advantage of me," I replied.

"And what action usually follows those thoughts?"

"Retaliation, through destructive words or actions."

"Exactly. Once you retaliate in any way- you lose."

Abe then pulled out a piece of paper and drew the following diagram:

Someone says, or does something, you don't like

↓

You interpret it as an attack or a threat

↓

Negative emotions; anger, hatred, resentment surface

↓

Fight or flight response activated

↓

You allow negative thoughts to control actions

↓

Adverse action taken against the other party; retaliation

↓

You lose

"Does this make sense?"

"It does, but how do you control your thoughts so you don't follow this path to failure?"

"Change how you interpret the words, or actions, of another. You have the absolute power to do that."

"Okay, but how do you handle an adverse situation where a person demeans you or does something immoral or unethical to you."

"First, never take anything personally. Remember, it's not about YOU. It's about the other party being unhappy about an event, a situation, or their life in general. When the other party performs an unethical or immoral act, you must understand they're a person of low character who regularly looks to hurt others to gain some type of advantage. By not personalizing it, you allow sound judgement to prevail over pride which also allows you to get a handle on your thoughts. You will more easily remember all the advantages you now possess, such as:

- Knowing that by keeping your composure, you are going to emerge on top.

- Self-control will allow you to effectively think through moments of turbulence and create positive choices; choices that will be productive rather than destructive.

- By exercising self-control, you show poise, restraint and are able to control the outcome better.

- You can use forgiveness as a way to shift the paradigm.

"So if you revisit the diagram I drew, by changing the interpretation, the message, you avoid the downward spiral resulting in sure defeat. And, finally, I've learned through experience what happens when you lose self-control:

- You bring more harm to yourself than you do to others.

- You create consternation for yourself, which brings about negative and wasted energy; energy that could be devoted to more important activities, such as working towards your defined purpose.

- You lose the respect of others around you, very likely impeding your ability to effectively lead. No person can properly lead without first controlling themselves.

- You lose valuable time. People obsess over the littlest things wasting valuable time they can never recover.

I found myself writing so fast and furiously, my hand began to hurt. I asked Abe to slow down a few times to make sure I captured all of this great information in my notes.

"Abe, I agree with all the things you are saying about staying on key, but it's difficult to accept when there are no consequences for a person who purposely and egregiously harms another. In other words, their actions go unpunished. How do you reconcile that?"

"How do you know their actions go unpunished? Remember the universe will return to you exactly what you deserve. If you choose to harm or take advantage of another, you will be penalized in the future for these adverse actions. That's what I believe. That's how I reconcile it. But never, under any circumstance, strike back, seek revenge or slander another person."

"Abe, you've probably been in thousands of negotiations where you've had to practice self-control. Do you find it difficult when the other party is being unreasonable?"

Negotiations

"Young man, the key to any successful negotiation is to arrive at an agreement where all parties walk away happy; a 'win-win.' That's very important if you ever want to negotiate again with the other party. In other words, if someone feels taken advantage of, they will refrain from working with or collaborating with you in the future. There were six critical points I followed in every negotiation.

"I know this lesson isn't about negotiations but would you mind sharing all six points?"

"Not at all…"

Controlling Your Emotions: You can't control another person's actions, however, you can control your own <u>reaction</u>. This means that if you remain in control of your emotions, you can control how you act or what you say. Never let another person bait you into losing control of your emotions.

Listen, Listen, Listen: Always remember to listen. By listening you'll discover and understand the other party's issues, problems and "hot buttons." Then, when you are finished listening, summarize what they've said so that everyone is on the same page.

See A Partner, Not An Enemy: In many instances, this may be difficult to do, especially when you are dealing with unreasonable people. However, the key in any negotiation is to reach a mutually satisfactory <u>agreement</u> so both sides are happy. It is much easier to accomplish this goal if you approach the negotiation with the perspective of creating a partner, rather than an opposing enemy. In a productive outcome both sides walk away happy and a long-term, mutually beneficial relationship is formed. If you finish a negotiation and receive everything you want and the other side feels like they did not; a future negotiation with that party is unlikely.

Preparation: If you want to be successful in your negotiation, prepare extensively. You get one chance to navigate the negotiation in the right direction. Make the most of that chance.

Don't Rush To The Finish: The closing is often characterized by a rush. Take your time. Allow the other party to digest the agreement. Sum up the agreement to make sure both sides have the same understanding.

Put it in Writing: We negotiate almost every day to reach a decision. When these decisions are made in the course of business, make sure they're in writing and signed by both parties.

Before we conclude today's lesson on self-control, or staying on key, I want you to remember when you find yourself in a disagreement or dispute...

- This is the time to pull out this powerful weapon
- Never, ever defend. Calmly stay on point and don't let the other party take you off course.

I thanked, Abe, as I always did, and we parted once again feeling like we had accomplished a lot. On the way home, however, it struck me that our time together was winding down and, for the first time, my euphoric feeling was tinged with a bit of sadness. I began treasuring his words and his camaraderie more than ever.

The Assignment

1) List 5 past experiences you've encountered where you've lost your self-control.

2) Next to each one of those 5 experiences, record how you would have handled each one differently, and what you learned from each.

Symphony No.19

Hitting the High Notes

"It's not the stresses on the outside that are the problems;
it's your internal environment not being able to handle them."

For my assignment, I found it easy to list five past experiences where I lost control of my emotions. Like Abe, when he was younger, I too possessed a short and unpredictable temper. But after hearing Abe's lesson, I was determined to master my negative reactions and emotions and never retaliate so that I might be victorious in the journey of conquering **self**!

It was actually quite cathartic to go back and record how I would handle each experience devoid of any acrimony. Reliving each experience felt real, like I was actually in the moment again; this time, handling the situation with more clarity, composure and grace. The ultimate outcome, at least on paper, was a 'win-win.'

As I made my way up to Abe's apartment, I couldn't tell if I was more excited to hear the 'clue' he always tossed me, or the lesson itself!"

"Hello, and good morning!" I said cheerfully.

"Good morning, young man. Did you take the elevator or the steps today?"

"The elevator," I replied with a grin, "I always take the elevator. It's twelve flights of steps. You'd know if I took the steps; I'd be huffing and puffing!"

"A young man like you? I doubt it!" he said with a chuckle. I was trying to find the clue; but came up empty-handed. *Clueless*, I thought to myself.

"How was your assignment?"

"Easy! Self-control was never one of my strengths, so compiling that list was a piece of cake! Ten minutes, at most," I said with a smirk. "However, reliving each experience was a little more painful...but good. I 'flipped the script' on each one and came up with a better way to handle it. Next time, thanks to you, I'll be able to do better..."

"Well done. Please share some of the experiences with me."

So, for the next twenty minutes, I shared a few stories with Abe and how I envisioned changing each one. They ranged from past work related incidents to the mishandling of bad service in restaurants and even experiences with inconsiderate drivers.

"Any guess for today's lesson?"

"I haven't the slightest idea...." I replied.

"Today we're going to 'hit the high notes' and talk about health, peace of mind and being in optimum condition."

"Oh-that's why you asked me if I took the elevator or steps." Abe smiled.

Pay Yourself First

"Nutrition, exercise, rest, mindset; they all play a huge role in determining how we feel. If we treat ourselves **well**, we feel great and have a much better chance at succeeding at whatever we choose. Being at your optimum health and peak performance requires attention, just like anything else in life. One way to think of it is by 'paying yourself first' with excellent self-care so that you have energy throughout your day.

People have a misguided idea that if we ignore our health, it will somehow take care of itself. No! Your wellness and your 'internal environment' is a direct reflection of your time invested in YOU and plays a major role in how we handle ongoing stressors. In fact, **it's not the stresses on the outside which are the problems, it's your internal environment not being able to handle them.**"

"What are you referring to when you speak of 'internal environment?" I asked.

"When I talk about your internal environment, I'm referring to how your mind and body are performing together. Think of it this way, when you feel tired, lethargic or ill, do you react the same way to an adverse event as you do when you feel relaxed, well-rested and healthy? Do you have as much tolerance and patience? Are you able to think with the same level of intensity and energy?"

"Not at all," I responded. "When I feel lethargic, my mind feels foggy and I have difficulty thinking through issues and potential problems to create viable solutions. Ideas don't flow seamlessly. I'm not as determined to achieve my goals and my anxiety level rises significantly. And, I tend to become overwhelmed more frequently. My tolerance for taking on tasks drops off greatly."

"Exactly! And, you are much more at risk to experience fear," Abe added, "and, as you just mentioned, you become overwhelmed more frequently, which is a byproduct of 'The Cycle of Fear.'

A Repertoire for Health:
1-REST

"For today's lesson I want to concentrate on three of the four components associated with a healthy mind, body and spirit." Abe stated. "First, let's begin with rest. Lack of rest imitates aging, so imagine how hard it is to focus when your brain hasn't had time to be rejuvenated? When your mind is fatigued, as you just mentioned, you're not thinking at peak performance. You're ingenuity and creativity are lacking, so your ability to generate new and exciting ideas is adversely affected. These ideas are necessary to help you accomplish your defined purposes.

My personal opinion is to get eight hours of sleep per night to function at peak performance the next day. Some people will be able to properly function with less and some need more, but eight is [on average] what you should strive for. Additionally, I believe in meditating twice a day, somewhere between 15 to 20 minutes, once in the morning and once in the early evening."

"I've never meditated," I responded. "Where do I start?

"I practice Transcendental Meditation, which requires some practice and some training. It allows my mind to achieve a state of inner peace and helps greatly to keep me calm. I recommend investigating this technique at some point in the future. But for right now, take some time this next month, as part of your assignment, and research different meditation techniques. Then choose one you find comfortable implementing."

"I'll start researching immediately. I'm also curious about Transcendental Meditation so I'll be researching that as well."

"I look forward to hearing about your discoveries in our next session."

"Abe, I'd like to revisit your opinion regarding eight hours of sleep each night. Sometimes I find it difficult to fall asleep at night, especially after a stressful day at the office and I'm lucky if I get six hours of sleep."

"That's why adding meditation in your daily routine is so important. It helps reinvigorate you and alleviate stress. Additionally, watch your breathing patterns during the day. As you get overwhelmed with stress and anxiety, your breathing tends to get rapid and short. Take deep slow breaths, which will help you relax and offset the stress you're experiencing. Here are several other recommendations I use to help me fall asleep faster and longer:

- I try not to eat anything during the week after 7:30 PM, especially foods that are rich and heavy. If I do, I find I don't sleep soundly and I awaken feeling lethargic.

- I read every night and rarely watch television before retiring for the evening.

- I begin mastering my day the night before when I create my list of action steps that need to be completed, organized in order of priority for the next day. It allows me to sleep better knowing I'm prepared and organized.

- I drink a great deal of water. However, I'm careful to not drink excessively after 7:30 PM so I don't awaken in the middle of the night to go to the bathroom.

- I keep to a set schedule by turning in at 10:00 PM and awakening at 6:00 AM.

- I keep a pen and pad of paper next to my bed so I can employ the power of self-suggestion when the next great idea or concept pops into my head. I write it down instantly to avoid having to remember it, which can trigger stress.

- I exercise daily.

2- EAT CLEAN

"The next component associated with a healthy mind, body and spirit is proper nutrition. Now, I'm not a nutritionist and I don't pretend to be one. These are only recommendations, which I've learned from my readings, research, and discussions with people in the wellness field. Plus, my own experience with food and how it makes me feel. Also, I believe one of the vital keys to feeling great is a healthy gut."

"A healthy gut?" My eyebrows went up.

"Yes, well- making sure that your gastrointestinal [or digestive system] is healthy and functioning normally. This is done by eating high-fiber foods, managing stress and taking the right supplements. Here's what I do…"

- I eat clean, all natural, preferably organic foods, without any artificial flavors or preservatives.

- I drink 5-8 glasses of filtered water every day. I never drink soft drinks, coffee or anything with added sugar. I also drink herbal teas.

- I juice daily using fresh organic fruits and vegetables. One in particular I enjoy is carrot- apple-spinach juice.

- I avoid simple, refined sugars.

- I also avoid fried foods.

- I prefer eating smaller meals more frequently, 5 or 6 times daily as opposed to 2 to 3 large meals.

- I avoid eating large lunches so that I don't feel lethargic during a work day.

- I eat whole grains and fruit rich in fiber. I tend to opt for gluten-free grains.

- I eat hormone-free natural proteins.

"As your mind is tied to your body, poor food choices can increase the likelihood of experiencing anxiety and depression."

"That's a pretty strict regimen you follow, Abe.

"I'm certainly not perfect. I deviate in moderation. My sweet tooth gets indulged occasionally on the weekends when we go out to dinner with friends and family. Once in a while, I eat less-than-healthy foods. But, again, it's all about the small steps that create macro results over time. I can tell the difference when I deviate from my regular nutrition plan; I don't feel as energetic or creative as I normally do."

3- MOVE MORE, SIT LESS

"The final part of today's lesson is staying active and exercising, especially for an old man like myself," Abe said with a grin.

"Abe, I'd hardly call you 'old' and you appear to be in very good shape!"

"Thank you. I exercise daily with a one hour brisk morning walk followed by some light stretching. If it's too cold or raining, I'll perform some calisthenics. I also spend about twenty minutes, three times a week, lifting light weights to maintain muscle mass and bone density. Movement is key to keep the blood circulating and forcing oxygen to the brain so that it may function at a high level. I prefer to perform my exercise routine in the morning to 'jump start' and energize me for the day."

"I do believe in exercising regularly, Abe. I always feel better exercising in the morning, especially strength training. It's a tremendous stress release."

"You'll find that the most successful people find time to live a healthy lifestyle." Abe stated. "There is a direct correlation with how we feel and how we perform both in business and in our personal life. If you feel great, you're much more likely to achieve success and experience healthier relationships."

"Sounds like a great assignment. I'll be curious to hear about the fourth component; mindset."

"Just wait, young man…you'll see next month," he said as he let me out the door.

The Assignment

- To research different meditation techniques and choose one you find comfortable implementing.

- To create/list 3 overall goals for your wellness [i.e.: 'Get to bed by 9:30 PM on the weekdays.' Or 'Lower my cholesterol by 40 points,' or 'Walk every morning before work.'

- Once defined, create three micro-goals to support them which can change weekly as you create a new habit/lifestyle.

- Record what works and what needs to be modified, and how you feel physically and emotionally.

Symphony No. 20

The Mental Maestro

"Everyone has within them the power to determine their ultimate destiny."

As I launched into the first part of my assignment, I found it was easy for me to grasp the nutrition and exercise part of the lesson. I've always believed in the power of these two tenets. In fact, I discovered the power of juicing back in the late 1980's after seeing an "info-merical" espousing the benefits of juicing natural fruits and vegetables. I've continued to juice almost every day for the last 25+ years.

Next, I explored different meditation techniques and chose a very simple method that I began practicing ten minutes a day, twice a day. First, I found a quiet place to sit comfortably without any distractions. Then, while sitting still, I focused on my breath. I took deep breaths and concentrated on just being in the present: the NOW. I noticed how I felt and the sounds around me. I struggled mightily at first! My mind would continuously wander, so to help neutralize this, I would concentrate on breathing deeply and slowly, counting to five on each breath in and again on each breath out. Over time, and with practice, my mind would wander less and less. [Years later, I branched out and discovered Transcendental Meditation, which I now practice twice a day, twenty minutes a day. I highly recommend learning this wonderful technique as it has helped me find the rest I need throughout the day and achieve a state of inner peace.]

Abe's words reinforcing consistency kept rolling around in my head. That was always the 'hitch'—*consistency!* There were weeks that I missed exercising due to a heavy work schedule and I was still eating simple, refined sugars such as breads and sweets. Once in a while, I was consuming fried foods. Less frequently still, I had large meals before bed.

So, I set out to exercise four mornings a week, [three during the week and once on the weekend], eliminate fried foods and minimize simple, refined sugars [such as desserts] to once on the weekends. I also stopped eating at 7:30 PM at night and ate smaller meals more frequently; usually five to six times throughout the day. Lastly, I eliminated all soft drinks and bottled fruit juices and replaced them with water.

At first, like everything else, these changes were difficult, especially reducing my intake of simple, refined sugars. However, as each day passed it became easier. Soon, all the benefits associated with proper nutrition and an effective exercise program were showing up:

a) More energy, less lethargy
b) A better, deeper sleep
c) More relaxed
d) Sharper clarity, less fogginess
e) Reduced anxiety and more tolerance for handling stressful situations
f) More regularity

As I came into Abe's apartment for our twentieth session, I was feeling pretty good.

"Good morning, Abe," I said.

"Good morning, young man. Are you in the right frame of mind to learn one of life's most important lessons?"

"Absolutely I am! I'm presuming that question was a prelude to today's lesson on mindset?"

"Indeed- you are correct! The final piece to our lesson on a healthy, mind, body and spirt is 'Having the Right Mindset.' Think of it like being a 'mental maestro,' if you will. I felt it deserved its own session because it's one of life's most important, if not the most important, lessons to master. But before we start today's lesson, how did you fare with your assignment?"

"Really well," I replied. I went on to tell him of all the ups and downs I went through to find a sustainable regime. He was particularly pleased with my simple meditation techniques and all the benefits I was experiencing as I became more consistent with exercise and nutrition.

Your Ultimate Destiny

"Here's the thing," Abe began, "everyone has within them the power to determine their ultimate destiny. The choice lies within! It's up to us to opt in to our own destiny. How you direct your mind, what you think, and what you ultimately magnetize and attract is up to you. Optimism and gratitude are conducive to success, while negativity and pessimism are conducive to failure. Even the greatest strategic plans cannot overcome a negative mindset. Only through positive thoughts can you attain total emotional freedom and the power to achieve whatever it is you desire.

The overwhelming majority of people live within very narrow limits, choosing to create their own self-made prisons. These prisons are created through the negative emotions of fear, worry, despondency, self-doubt which manifests into avoidance. Over time, this upside-down thinking accumulates and –viola; people are mystified as to why they have arrived at a certain place in their lives."

"Abe, in our previous lessons you've discussed how most people allow negative thoughts to control the majority of their thinking and thus create their future. If this is due to many years of improper thinking, how do you suddenly change? Where do you start?"

Orchestrating Your Thoughts

Awareness

"The first key is awareness. You must be aware of your thoughts. The reason for this is you're not going to be able to stop thinking. In other words, if you have the same thought over and over again, you can't just tell yourself to stop. It doesn't work that way. Thoughts only can change and influence your actions when backed by an underlying emotion."

"How do you get to that underlying emotion?" I asked.

"By tracking your thoughts over a period of time and analyzing them. Then, you will be able to see a pattern. For example: 'Did I say something wrong in the meeting? If I don't impress my client today, will they replace me? Did my children get to school on time? Are they okay? Is the pain in my side this morning a sign of a disease?' And so on..." Then Abe asked, "What do all these thoughts have in common?"

"They're all based on fear and worry," I responded.

"Exactly. So if you can control the emotions, the thoughts have no traction."

"Do you record every thought during the day?" I asked.

"No," Abe said with a smile, "you'd never get anything done. I recommend scheduling one fifteen- minute- period, twice a day for the next 30 days; preferably at the same time every day. Check in with your thoughts and then write them down in a journal or diary. You'll start to notice a pattern pretty quickly."

"What will this pattern show me? I asked.

"What the core emotion is and, therefore, the source of your thought patterns. Is it fear, worry, anger, jealousy, guilt?" Then ask yourself where that emotion came from and why it exists. What is causing this emotion to attach to these thoughts and control your destiny? And, if its negative, why are you letting that thought take up real estate in your brain? Once you recognize the emotion, then you deal with it directly using the tools we've discussed in our previous lessons.

Wellness Within

"Next, remember the main point from our last lesson; it's not the stresses on the outside that are the problems, it's your internal environment not being able to handle them. We actually need stress, as a tool for resilience. Its ongoing stress that isn't good. How your body feels affects your mind; they are not separate. When you feel great, negative thoughts pass by much faster without much affect or traction."

[One of the keys to managing my stress is controlling my internal environment. When I eat well, exercise and meditate regularly, negative thoughts pass by quickly without adversely impacting me.]

Self-Talk

"Self–talk is another way to move away from any self-made prisons and will help you achieve total emotional freedom. Remember in our lesson on courage, we discussed self-talk and positive affirmations. Saturate yourself with affirmations like these…"

✓ I've already succeeded and ready to accomplish more.

✓ There are no limits! The world is full of unlimited resources, waiting for me to claim them.

✓ I don't believe in defeat.

✓ I have the ability to think: everything I need to be successful.

✓ I live my life honestly and with integrity so nature will guide me in the right direction.

✓ Every day, and every way, I'm getting closer to my goal.

✓ Every setback is just another learning experience; necessary to achieve my final goal.

Good self-talk will help steer your mind away from self-sabotaging thoughts and towards ones that will serve you.

Prayer

"In our lesson on Gratitude, we discussed the power of prayer and how in times of turmoil or confusion, it can help guide you to make difficult decisions. The most important factor in any defined purpose is one's belief about it."

Words Create Worlds

"Negative, internal messages clutter the mind and overtime build up to create a feeling of despondency leading you on a path to nowhere. You must root them out by paying attention to your thoughts and stopping them in their tracks. Make a list of the negative words and phrases that keep coming back to you and then see if you can determine their genesis. Then ask yourself- are these thoughts working for me or not?"

- I'm afraid.
- What if this happens?
- I'm so tired.
- Why is this always happening to me?
- I can't do that.
- It's so hard.
- I've had it.
- I knew this was going to happen.
- Why me?
- I can't catch a break.
- If I didn't have bad luck I wouldn't have any luck at all.

Review this list continually and when these negative internal messages occur, change them to a positive statement. For example, 'I'm so tired,' to 'I have unlimited energy and will see this through.' [See the next page for a general list of positive statements/action steps.]

Instead, say…

- ✓ I am going to enrich the lives of at least three people today.
- ✓ I will use the 'Power of Gratitude' to off-set any disabling thoughts.
- ✓ I will use my gift of grace and forgiveness often.
- ✓ Happiness is found in the NOW!
- ✓ Mistakes are only setbacks if you allow them to be.
- ✓ I will take the right action in the present.
- ✓ My business will be an extended shadow of me and my values.
- ✓ I will be a leader with a message, not one with a grievance.
- ✓ Imagination + courage=the ultimate power.
- ✓ I will appreciate every second of the day.
- ✓ I will build my future one thought at a time.
- ✓ I will not let a negative mindset drive any part of my life.
- ✓ I will not be a prisoner to my past.
- ✓ I will dream big and leave a lasting legacy for generations to remember.

Seeing is Believing

"If you can see it, you can achieve it! Visualization is a very powerful tool. Use it liberally to imprint on your mind what you DO want, not what you DON'T. It will help change your mindset from negative to positive and then you will see more clearly your successful outcome. You will, over time, be able to overcome any obstacle life puts in front of you. And, before I provide the next assignment, I want to share with you a great proverb from Ben Franklin, which I hope you'll find useful. In 1758 Benjamin Franklin wrote the classic essay *The Way to Wealth*. The essay's advice is based on the themes of work ethic and frugality, but I also believe it's a great lesson on the right mindset. In the essay there is a story about a great number of people who are at an auction of merchants' goods where they are lamenting the heavy taxes being imposed upon them. Father Abraham then stands up..."

The Story of Father Abraham

An old man named Father Abraham stood up and said, "Friends, the taxes are indeed very heavy, and, if those laid on by the government were the only ones we had to pay, we might more easily discharge them; but we have many others, and much more grievous to some of us. We are taxed twice as much by our idleness, three times as much by our pride, and four times as much by our folly; and from these taxes the commissioners cannot ease or deliver us, by allowing an abatement."

"For the most part, we cannot control what our others do or don't do. But what we can control are the choices we make for ourselves. Fear and worry, indecision and doubt, envy, greed, jealousy, anger, hatred, laziness, afraid of change, unwilling to forgive, poor character, lack of independent thinking; these are the taxes much more grievous to you. And these are the taxes you and only you impose on yourself. You have a lot of work to do this month, but it's very important to have a right mindset to be successful and have a happy life."

"I get it! I look forward to the assignment."

"Put everything you have into this assignment as it will be your last."

"My last?"

"You've successfully learned the twenty 'symphonies' to guide you to a successful, fruitful and happy life… and I'm very proud of your commitment. So our next meeting will be our last and we'll review the principles we talked about. Hopefully, I can leave you with some final words of wisdom," he said with a smile. "By no means will this be our last conversation. I want you to keep in touch with me and let me know how things are going and all your achievements."

"You know I will…"

"See you next month!"

The Assignment

1) Schedule two 15 minute times a day for the next 30 days, preferably at the same time every day, when you do nothing but be aware of your thoughts and then write them down in a journal or diary.

2) Review and analyze the list and determine the underlying emotion.

3) Once the emotion is determined deal with it directly using the tools we've discussed in previous lessons.

4) Root out the negatives. Make a list of the negative internal messages and start changing them to positive statements.

Our Final Encore

"Leave a lasting legacy for generations to remember."

The drive was a lot different from the other twenty-some trips. Although I was excited about this final lesson, I knew it would be my last and, with that, came a sense of loss. Two years! What an incredible journey! My thoughts turned to how everyone could receive this kind of knowledge and how I could deliver these lessons everywhere. I was still mulling that idea over as I came into Abe's spectacular library for the last time. I noticed where I typically sit for our sessions he had laid out at least two dozen classic books on the desk.

"Abe, what are all these books?" He looked and said, "These are for you. They've served me well over the years. Read them! I'm passing these classics onto you as a reminder of the importance of all of the lessons you've learned over the past two years. I trust you'll put them to good use and one day you'll pay it forward."

What an incredible gift! I felt honored and humbled, and to this day, I've read every one and continue to use them as a reminder of the importance of the lessons I've learned.

"Since in this session we will be reviewing the previous twenty lessons, I have no special lead-ins; no 'clues' today. But, before we start, tell me how you fared with your assignment?"

"Wonderful and much needed. Every day I schedule two fifteen -minute periods to just be aware of my thoughts and then write them down in my journal. I noticed a pattern of negative thoughts based around the words "what if." 'What if we don't meet our projections this month?' 'What if the stock market continues to drop?' And so on….."

"What were the underlying emotions?"

"Fear and worry." I replied.

"How did you overcome these emotions?"

"Positive affirmations, prayer and a belief and faith that everything will be just fine as long as I continue to persevere without hesitation towards my defined purposes and continue to enrich the lives of those around me. I now believe wholeheartedly in this combination. There is a world full of abundant opportunities and to concern myself about anything that hasn't happened yet, is pointless. As you say- don't worry about debts that may never come due. I also noticed a reoccurring pattern of concocting stories in my mind of retaliation towards people who have wronged me. I never realized, until I took part in this exercise, my tendency to do that! In some respects, I probably spent more time thinking about those scenarios than I did with the *what ifs…*"

"That's a great discovery. What were the underlying emotions?"

"Anger and resentment."

"How did you overcome those emotions?"

"I remembered our lesson on forgiveness and how grace is forgiveness without requiring the other person to ask. I know now how draining and debilitating it can be to harbor negative energy. So, I am working on releasing it. I went back to that lesson [and the assignment] and I replayed the stories, this time visualizing forgiving each person while I shook their hand and smiled, saying the words, 'I forgive you for your past indiscretions towards me.' "

"Excellent."

"Lastly, in order to root out all the negative internal messages, I created a list. The two most common by far were 'I'm so tired' and 'I've had it,' which occurred anytime I became overwhelmed. To counteract the negative messages, I changed them to 'I have lots of energy to deal with this' and 'I just learned something new to help me succeed in the future.' "

"Again, outstanding work. You're putting our lessons to great use. This is a terrific prelude to what I wanted to cover today…I would be honored if you would summarize our journey and what you've learned over the past two years."

So, I pulled out my binder of notes and began talking about all of the incredible lessons and principles I learned over the past two years, how they affected my life, how I would continue to apply them in the future and most importantly how I will pass them on to anyone willing to dedicate the time to learning them to better their life.

"You've learned well, my son. I'm very proud of your hard work and dedication and especially your desire to share this information with the world. Now let me conclude our journey with a poem I love..." He proceeded to pull out a framed sheet of paper out of his desk drawer. He read me the following poem by Robert Frost.

The Road Not Taken

Two roads diverged in a yellow wood,
And sorry I could not travel both
And be one traveler, long I stood
And looked down one as far as I could
To where it bent in the undergrowth;

Then took the other, as just as fair,
And having perhaps the better claim
Because it was grassy and wanted wear,
Though as for that the passing there
Had worn them really about the same,

And both that morning equally lay
In leaves no step had trodden black.
Oh, I kept the first for another day!
Yet knowing how way leads on to way
I doubted if I should ever come back.

I shall be telling this with a sigh
Somewhere ages and ages hence:
Two roads diverged in a wood, and I,
I took the one less traveled by,
And that has made all the difference.

"Now go out and forge your own path," Abe said "by taking the road less traveled. Make your own decisions without fear and know that no obstacle can stop you from succeeding. You're a man of great character who listens well. It has been my pleasure teaching you and passing on the philosophies and beliefs that have served me so well over my life. Take these lessons and share them with the world so that, when it is your time to leave, you will have left a lasting legacy."

And, with that, it was over. You might think I got tired of listening to opera, or Abe calling me, 'young man.' But I am here to tell you, I never did. Thanks to Abe, we have an everlasting masterpiece; a gift which will stand the test of time.

About the Author

Mark Luterman

Mark is CEO of Primax Ventures, LLC, a company devoted to helping business owners around the country prosper and achieve their desired goals. He is a speaker, author, motivator, teacher and coach. He steadfastly believes anyone, with the right techniques and mindset, can create unlimited success. Mark has been hailed as the true "Business Secret Weapon" by business owners, partners, and associations nationwide.

Mark had a career as a financial advisor/CPA in Public Accounting for 11 years before entering private industry in1996 to become a part owner of a consumer cleaning products manufacturer. Over the next 10 years, the company became a nationally known brand name and one of the leaders in their industry. In October of 2005, the company was sold.

Subsequent to the sale of the company, Mark co-founded a regional sports media and publishing company that publishes a monthly sports newspaper, has a weekend television program, and an interactive website supplying up-to-date information on professional, college and high school sports.

For three years, Mark hosted and produced a weekly radio show heard on CBS radio called *The Small Business Secret Weapon Hour,* a show packed with tips and strategies for success minded business owners. He has been a guest on television and other radio shows and a contributor to various business and newspaper publications.

In addition to *Abe's Final Masterpiece* –available on Amazon- Mark has authored *6 Simple Steps to Starting Your Own Business, The 5 Secret Weapon Steps to Unlimited Prosperity* and the 8 CD set *Mark Luterman's Ultimate Roadmap to Creating a Thriving Business.*

He is the proud father of Lindsay and Matthew and husband to his wife Bobbie.

Find out more at www.markluterman.com; or one of these links:
Facebook: https://www.facebook.com/MarkLutermanSBSW
Twitter: https://twitter.com/markluterman
LinkedIn: https://www.linkedin.com/in/mark-luterman-66121531
YouTube: https://www.youtube.com/user/thesecretweaponman

Suggested Reading

The Prosperity Bible: a collection of nineteen of the greatest writings of all time on the secrets to wealth and prosperity. It includes:

1. *Think and Grow Rich* by Napoleon Hill

2. *Acres of Diamonds* by Russell Conwell

3. *A Message to Garcia* by Elbert Hubbard

4. *As a Man Thinketh* by James Allen

5. *The Game of Life and How to Play It* by Florence Scovel Shinn

6. *The Science of Getting Rich* by Wallace Wattles

7. *Creative Mind and Success* by Ernest Holmes

8. *Prosperity* by Charles Fillmore

9. *In Tune With the Infinite* by Ralph Waldo Trine

10. *The Master Key System* by Charles Haanel

11. *The Secret of Success* by William Walker Atkinson

12. *The Art of Money Getting* by P.T Barnum

13. *The Way to Wealth* by Benjamin Franklin

14. *The Secret of The Ages* by Robert Collier

15. *The Conquest of Poverty* by Helen Wilmans

16. *How to Attract Success* by F.W. Sears

17. *The Power of Concentration* by Theron Q. Dumont

18. *How to Grow Success* by Elizabeth Towne

19. *The Mental Equivalent* by Emmett Fox

More...

The Greatest Salesman in the World by Og Mandino

The Greatest Salesman in the World Part II by Og Mandino

The Law of Success by Napoleon Hill

Earl Nightengale's Greatest Discovery by Earl Nightengale

Your Subconscious Power by Charles M. Simmons

The Richest Man in Babylon by George S. Clason

Essay on Compensation by Ralph Waldo Emerson

The Ultimate Gift by Jim Stovall

How to Stop Worrying and Start Living by Dale Carnegie

Good to Great by Jim Collins

Influence by Robert B. Cialdini

Made in the USA
Middletown, DE
04 November 2022